BERNARD SHAW

A Critical View

Nicholas Grene

*Fellow and Director of Studies in Modern English
Trinity College, Dublin*

M

**MACMILLAN
PRESS**

First edition 1984
Reprinted 1987

Published by
THE MACMILLAN PRESS LTD
Houndmills, Basingstoke, Hampshire RG21 2XS
and London
Companies and representatives
throughout the world

Printed in Hong Kong

British Library Cataloguing in Publication Data
Grene, Nicholas
Bernard Shaw.—(Macmillan Studies in Anglo-Irish
literature)
I. Shaw, Bernard
I. Title
822'.912   PR 5367
ISBN 0–333–33424–8 (hardcover)
ISBN 0–333–43538–9 (paperback)

BERNARD SHAW
A Critical View

MACMILLAN STUDIES IN ANGLO-IRISH LITERATURE

Maeve Good
W. B. YEATS AND THE CREATION OF A TRAGIC
  UNIVERSE

Nicholas Grene
BERNARD SHAW: A CRITICAL VIEW

John O'Riordan
A GUIDE TO O'CASEY'S PLAYS

Paul Scott Stanfield
YEATS AND POLITICS IN THE 1930s

Also by Nicholas Grene

SYNGE: A CRITICAL STUDY OF THE PLAYS
SHAKESPEARE, JONSON, MOLIÈRE: THE COMIC
  CONTRACT
THE WELL OF THE SAINTS by J. M. Synge (*editor*)

Series Standing Order

If you would like to receive future titles in this series as they
are published, you can make use of our standing order
facility. To place a standing order please contact your
bookseller or, in case of difficulty, write to us at the address
below with your name and address and the name of the
series. Please state with which title you wish to begin your
standing order. (If you live outside the UK we may not have
the rights for your area, in which case we will forward your
order to the publisher concerned.)

Standing Order Service, Macmillan Distribution Ltd,
Houndmills, Basingstoke, Hampshire, RG21 2XS, England.

For my mother and father

Contents

Preface

Is Bernard Shaw, if not 'better than Shakespeare', the second greatest playwright in the English language? It remains very much a question, even though in the view of many Shavians it ought to be beyond dispute. And on the face of it, it is hard to dispute. Shaw's plays now, more than thirty years after his death, a hundred and thirty years after his birth, continue to be read and played all over the world. If he is not the second greatest playwright in English, who is? There is no other dramatist who has produced such an enduring canon of major plays, or so many playable minor ones; no one but Shakespeare can match him in the sheer range of stage characters created. A recent critic has shown that, in England at least, Shaw is by far the most frequently performed dramatist after Shakespeare.[1] And yet a remarkable number of educated and literate people, even people with a special interest in the drama, would receive with astonishment or dismiss with contempt the claim that Shaw was Shakespeare's nearest rival. For years it was commonplace to deny that he was a playwright at all, and still there remains a widespread feeling that his characters are little more than walking ideas manipulated by a preacher/propagandist. His reputation in university departments of English or drama is extremely limited; his name appears very infrequently on course syllabuses and few academics would place him as one of the great writers of the twentieth century. While the standing of Joyce, Lawrence, Yeats and Eliot becomes more assured with every year, Shaw continues to suffer from a disabling association with cranks and enthusiasts, a general aura of vegetarianism and all-wool clothing, outmoded Fabian socialism and even more outmoded Creative Evolutionism.

Shaw has not wanted for able and devoted disciples who have made it their business to try to combat these prejudices. Scholars such as Dan Laurence and Stanley Weintraub have given their best energies to the serious work of chronicling and documenting his achievement. Critics from Eric Bentley on have tried to demonstrate the substance and significance of his work either by analysis of his skills as a playwright or by the exposition of his ideas or both. Many of them have added measurably to our understanding and respect for Shaw – one thinks, for instance, of Martin Meisel's excellent book on Shaw and nineteenth-century theatre.[2] And yet modern Shaw criticism on the whole has tended to suffer from its defensiveness, its need to demonstrate the value of his work in the face of disparagement and neglect. Again and again we find Shaw critics making what amount to professions of faith: a defiant introduction 'on taking Shaw seriously', a solemn commitment to the belief in Shaw's greatness, a self-conscious claim for Shaw's status as a great world teacher.[3] 'The time has not yet come', wrote Eric Bentley in 1947, 'to write unpolemically about Shaw.'[4] Surely by now that time has come, and we can afford to look critically at Shaw's limitations without feeling that we are selling out to his detractors.

It is as such an unpolemic, unapologetic critical study that this book is intended. I am not a professed card-carrying Shavian. I write out of mixed feelings about Shaw: admiration and annoyance, enjoyment and dissatisfaction, fascination and dislike. But I think that mixed feelings of this kind are more representative of reader and audience reaction to Shaw than the unreserved appreciation of more committed critics, who often appear to be preaching to the converted. Shaw is a playwright of quite extraordinary gifts – nothing in my view could be more mistaken than the old charge that he is not really a dramatist. And yet with all these gifts, why does he so often seem less than fully satisfying, even at his best? What sort of dramatic reality is represented by his distinctive form of comedy of ideas? Why do his slighter and less ambitious plays – *Arms and the Man*, say, or *Pygmalion* – sometimes seem more assured in their success than his major works? To what extent did he develop a real tragic vision in later plays such as *Heartbreak House* and *Saint Joan*? The book that follows is an attempt to articulate answers to these questions, to redefine the nature of Shaw's dramatic achievement by a critical analysis of both his strengths and limitations.

Acknowledgements

Grateful acknowledgement is made to the Society of Authors on behalf of the Bernard Shaw Estate for permission to quote from Shaw's work. Most of the quotations are taken from the following texts (abbreviated references in square brackets):

The Bodley Head Bernard Shaw: Collected Plays with Their Prefaces
(London, 1970–4), 7 vol [CP, I–VII].
Collected Letters, 1874–1897, edited by Dan H. Laurence
(London, 1965) [CL, I].
Collected Letters, 1898–1910, edited by Dan H. Laurence (London, 1972) [CL, II].

All other references are given in full in the notes.

My wife Eleanor Grene, my father David Grene, and my colleague Terence Brown have read parts or all of this book in manuscript. For their help and encouragement I am very grateful.

N.G.

1 Two Models: Wilde and Ibsen

Without the contribution of Irishmen there would scarcely be a single major comedy in English between 1700 and 1900. Farquhar, Goldsmith, Sheridan, Wilde – the Irish monopoly on eighteenth - and nineteenth-century comedy is remarkable. What is more, these Irish-English comedies have much in common. Each of the comedians was skilled at giving the London audience what they wanted, to some extent even what they expected, but with a cynical stylishness or a cut of satire which made their plays look strikingly original, and differentiated them from their blander English contemporaries. Aimwell in *The Beaux' Stratagem*, for instance, fulfils the ideal of early eighteenth-century tastes in his conversion to marriage for love; but his co-conspirator Archer remains faithful to the tougher ethics of the rake, and the 'happy divorce' of the Sullens, balancing the happy marriage of Aimwell at the end, lends piquancy to the play as a whole. Sheridan, on the other hand, professed to run counter to the tastes of his time in sending up the hypocrisies of sentimentalism in *The School for Scandal*. Yet the ending, with the revelation of Sir Peter's heart of gold reforming an only mildly erring Lady Teazle, is as properly sentimental as can be. Wilde, the last of the line, could produce 'woman with a past' plots of unimpeachable Victorian conventionality, and yet lace them with a series of epigrams which imply a totally cynical disbelief in the values the plots appear to endorse.

It is tempting to define this common quality of creative double-thinking as characteristically Irish. Farquhar, Sheridan, Goldsmith and Wilde may be seen as Irishmen in London out to make their way – aware of their provinciality, eager to succeed in metropolitan terms, but using their sense of distance and self-possession to cultivate a non-English audacity of style.[1] Such generalisations about nationality must not be pressed too hard, if only because of the obvious exceptions. Steele, as Irish as the others, produced plays utterly unambiguous in their humourless sentimentality. Sheridan was an orator and entrepreneur in an age of orators and entrepreneurs, and we should not lean too heavily on the idea of him as a fluent Irish talker winning his way to the managership of Drury Lane. However, the concept of the Irishman playing to a foreign market, what Joyce called the role of 'court jester to the English',[2] is genuinely there in the work of all the major Anglo-Irish comedians.

Shaw in many ways fits easily on to the end of this series – Farquhar, Goldsmith, Sheridan, Wilde. Like the rest of them, he came to London from an Anglo-Irish Protestant background, though lower down the social scale than some of the others. Like Wilde, in particular, he made his name as a personality long before he became a playwright. Indeed like so many of his Anglo-Irish comic predecessors, he turned to the writing of plays not as a full-time career, but as the occasional employment of an otherwise busy man. The style, the paradoxes, the wit relate him very obviously to Wilde. And yet his own feelings about Wilde and this whole Irish comic tradition are ambivalent. In some ways if there was one thing of which Shaw was certain at the outset of his career as a dramatist, it was that he would not be another mere Irish jester. He might use his Irish persona, his reputation for cynical iconoclasm, but he would use it to more pointed purpose than the Farquhars, Sheridans and Wildes. Shaw was not just out to conquer London, but to change London. And in this he took as precedent not the part of the Irish jester but that of the Scandinavian prophet. One way of approaching Shaw is by looking at two possible models for his work, the two most significant figures on the theatre scene in the 1890s when he was a reviewer and began writing plays: Wilde and Ibsen.

In a self-drafted interview in the *Star* in 1892, Shaw made clear both his sense of affinity with Wilde and his sense of difference. The interviewer was made to ask whether the public could expect any of Shaw's celebrated humour in *Widowers' Houses*, then about to be produced by the Independent Theatre:

> "Certainly not. I have removed with the greatest care every line that could possibly provoke a smile. I have been greatly misunderstood in this matter. Being an Irishman, I do not always see things exactly as an Englishman would: consequently my most serious and blunt statements sometimes raise a laugh and create an impression that I am intentionally jesting. I admit that some Irishmen do take advantage of the public in this way.

Wilde, unquestionably the ablest of our dramatists, has done so in 'Lady Windermere's Fan'. There are lines in that play which were put in for no other purpose than to make the audience laugh."

"'Widowers' Houses' will be quite free from that sort of thing, then?"

"Absolutely. However, I do not blame Wilde. He wrote for the stage as an artist. I am simply a propagandist."

(CP, I, 126–7)

A piece of Shaw's deadpan clowning like this has to be recognised for what it is. Naming Wilde as 'unquestionably the ablest of our dramatists', at that stage on the strength of *Lady Windermere's Fan* only, was no doubt intended to outrage and startle. It would be ludicrous to take literally Shaw's distinction between Wilde as artist and himself as propagandist. But from the (nearly simultaneous) beginning of their playwriting careers Shaw stressed the common distinctiveness of their Irish alienation and claimed for himself a greater responsibility in its use.

Shaw was clearly delighted with the subversion of seriousness which he found in *An Ideal Husband*, as we can see from his review of the first production in 1895.

In a certain sense Mr Wilde is to me our only thorough playwright. He plays with everything: with wit, with philosophy, with drama, with actors and audience, with the whole theatre. Such a feat scandalises the Englishman, who can no more play with wit and philosophy than he can with a football or cricket bat.

Shaw congratulates Wilde on the 'subtle and pervading levity' of *An Ideal Husband* because it annoys the English. There is no mistaking the tone of self-identification in his praise for Wilde here:

to the Irishman (and Mr Wilde is almost as acutely Irish an Irishman as the Iron Duke of Wellington) there is nothing in the world quite so exquisitely comic as an Englishman's seriousness. It becomes tragic, perhaps, when the Englishman acts on it; but that occurs too seldom to be taken into account, a fact which intensifies the humor of the situation, the total result being the Englishman utterly unconscious of his real self, Mr Wilde keenly

observant of it and playing on the self-unconsciousness with
irresistible humour, and finally, of course, the Englishman
annoyed with himself for being amused at his own expense, and
for being unable to convict Mr Wilde of what seems an obvious
misunderstanding of human nature.[3]

Shaw's claim for the Irish comedian, for both Wilde and himself, is
that they are capable of seeing the truth of English behaviour as the
Englishman cannot, that their comedy derives from the tongue-
in-cheek observation of the absurdities of the English social scene.
   Yet, remarkably, in view of his eloquent review of *An Ideal
Husband*, Shaw was disappointed in Wilde's final comic achievement, *The Importance of Being Earnest*. Of course, as always with
Shaw's reviewing, we need to allow for an element of perversity. His
contention that *The Importance* was an early play – 'it must certainly
have been written before Lady Windermere's Fan' – is an attempt
to make fools of the critics who declared that 'The Importance of
Being Earnest is a strained effort of Mr Wilde's at ultra-modernity,
and that it could never have been written but for the opening up of
entirely new paths in drama last year by Arms and the Man'.[4] But
his refusal to join in the chorus of praise for *The Importance* was not
just an affectation of singularity. He did not like the play – he was to
dislike it all his life – and the reasons why are significant:

> I cannot say that I greatly cared for The Importance of Being
> Earnest. It amused me, of course; but unless comedy touches me
> as well as amuses me, it leaves me with a sense of having wasted
> my evening. I go to the theatre to be moved to laughter, not to be
> tickled or bustled into it; and that is why, though I laugh as much
> as anybody at a farcical comedy, I am out of spirits before the end
> of the second act, and out of temper before the end of the third,
> my miserable mechanical laughter intensifying these symptoms
> at every outburst.[5]

It is curious to find Shaw, so often accused of heartless comedy
himself, complaining of want of feeling in Wilde. It was Shaw's *Arms
and the Man*, produced in 1894, which provoked Yeats's famous
dream of the sewing-machine that smiled. But Shaw's belief that
comedy should 'move to laughter' is basic to his work. For most
modern critics *The Importance* is Wilde's most perfect play, where he
finally liberated himself from the need to produce the convention-

ally sentimental plot to house his farcical vision of the absurd. To Shaw, the complete removal of an emotional strand from comedy, however conventional that emotion might have been, represented a step backwards towards the merely mechanical and unreal.

Shaw and Wilde never became friends. When recalling his memories of Wilde for the benefit of Frank Harris in 1916, Shaw could remember no more than half a dozen occasions on which they met. There was a social dimension to their mutual uneasiness, as Shaw told Harris:

> I was in no way predisposed to like him: he was my fellow-townsman, and a very prime specimen of the sort of fellow-townsman I most loathed: to wit, the Dublin snob. His Irish charm, potent with Englishmen, did not exist for me; and on the whole it may be claimed for him that he got no regard from me that he did not earn.[6]

It may be that Shaw was hurt by Wilde's famous epigram about him; at least he answered it with dignity in a letter to Ellen Terry: 'Oscar Wilde said of me "An excellent man: he has no enemies; and none of his friends like him." And that's quite true: they don't like me; but they are my friends, and some of them love me' (CL, 1, 668). The lack of a close relationship between them did not stop Shaw from supporting Wilde loyally during and after his imprisonment, and his one substantial essay on Wilde, published in German in the *Neue Freie Presse* in 1905, accords him generous praise. Yet in that essay it is clear what he saw as their essential differences and ultimately Wilde's limitation:

> On the whole, Wilde's tastes were basically different from mine. He loved luxury, and the salon and the *atelier* were his domain; while I was a man of the street, an agitator, a vegetarian, a teetotaler, incapable of enjoying the life of the drawing-room and the chatter of the studio.[7]

Shaw concludes that 'his originality lay in his superiority to the delusive morality of our time' but that 'he had not, as Nietzsche had, thought through his own situation sufficiently to understand himself. Without a precisely mapped-out program of life it is impossible, if not useless, to discard moral concepts.'[8]

Shaw's admiration for Wilde was qualified by his view of him as

essentially an unmodern writer: 'it is difficult to believe that the
author of An Ideal Husband was a contemporary of Ibsen,
Strindberg, Wagner, Tolstoi, or myself.'[9] In his section on
'Evolution in the Theatre' in the Preface to *Back to Methusaleh*, Shaw
names Wilde as the last of a comic tradition which began in the
seventeenth century:

> From Molière to Oscar Wilde we had a line of comedic
> playwrights who, if they had nothing fundamentally positive to
> say, were at least in revolt against falsehood and imposture, and
> were not only, as they claimed, 'chastening morals by ridicule',
> but, in Johnson's phrase, clearing our minds of cant, and thereby
> shewing an uneasiness in the presence of error which is the surest
> symptom of intellectual vitality. (CP, V, 335)

But these negative virtues were not enough:

> Ever since Shakespear, playwrights have been struggling with
> their lack of positive religion. Many of them were forced to
> become mere pandars and sensation-mongers because, though
> they had higher ambitions, they could find no better subject
> matter. From Congreve to Sheridan they were so sterile in spite of
> their wit that they did not achieve between them the output of
> Molière's single lifetime; and they were all (not without reason)
> ashamed of their profession, and preferred to be regarded as mere
> men of fashion with a rakish hobby. (CP, V, 336)

In a passage like this we see expressed the full Puritanism of Shaw
which ultimately differentiated him from Wilde, or indeed most
other comedians. For all his clowning, he believed that plays and
playwrights had to take themselves seriously, that they had to have
something positive to say. This was not necessarily to claim that all
plays should have a direct social or moral purpose, but that the
dramatist should feel himself committed to his work, not a 'mere
man of fashion with a rakish hobby'. It is this which made Shaw
reject Wilde's dandy-like aestheticism, and it is this which makes all
his own plays in some sense plays for Puritans.

The influence of Ibsen on Shaw is well known, and has by now
been often and thoroughly discussed.[10] J. L. Wisenthal has
collected all of Shaw's writings on Ibsen, including *The Quintessence
of Ibsenism*, and has shown in his introductory essay how much more

complex Shaw's response was than has generally been imagined.[11] Shaw did not butcher Ibsen to make a Fabian holiday; though *The Quintessence* was avowedly written to show what Ibsen had to offer socialists, it does not mean that it was all Shaw thought Ibsen had to offer. What Shaw rightly detected in Ibsen, and was most crucial for him, was a radical belief in artistic truth-telling that went far beyond any party-political platform. Ibsen spent most of his life avoiding identification with any political group and was particularly scornful of so-called progressive parties. His iconoclasm was not to be put to the service of a given set of social objectives. But that it was iconoclasm, and that Shaw was more nearly right about Ibsen than is normally supposed, is evident, for example, from Ibsen's comment in a letter about *Ghosts* before it was published: '*Ghosts* will probably cause alarm in some circles; but there is nothing to be done about it. If it didn't do that, there would have been no need to write it.'[12] Ibsen saw his own work, as Shaw saw it, as a contribution to a forward struggle to give people new images of truth, images which at first they would inevitably be unable to accept.

For Shaw Ibsen was the realist who at last enabled the theatre to escape from the vapid and meaningless ideals which had dominated it for so long. In *The Quintessence* he explains the unorthodox use he makes of the terms realist and idealist. The idealist is the man who creates self-deceiving myths to make tolerable the reality of a life which he could not otherwise endure. The realist insists on the liberation of the human will from the artificial constraints of idealism which he rejects as deadening and unreal. He is prepared to face life objectively without the narcotics of the ideal. It can be fairly objected that this view of Ibsen as realist suits some plays more than others, and does not take into account Ibsen's deeply ambiguous attitude towards idealistic self-sacrifice. But it explains why Shaw so constantly stressed the modernity of Ibsen, and saw him as a crucial revolutionary writer along with Nietzsche or Schopenhauer. In Shaw's evolutionary concept of human culture Ibsen is one of the 'pioneers of the march to the plains of heaven', moving forward the ideas of the race by destroying outmoded pieties and beliefs. It is in this spirit that Shaw celebrated Ibsen's 'plays of nineteenth-century life with which he overcame Europe, and broke the dusty windows of every dry-rotten theatre in it from Moscow to Manchester' (CP, v, 336).

If Ibsen is to be seen as a pioneer, a progressive in this suprapolitical sense, then the structure of his plays involves a dialectic of progressive understanding for an audience. Obviously here *A Doll's House* and *Ghosts* are Shaw's best examples. *A Doll's House* takes Nora, and us with her, from 'the sweet home, the womanly woman, the happy family life of the idealist's dream' through disillusionment to the determination to meet the real world and 'to find out its reality for herself'. *Ghosts*, which Shaw was one of the first to see as a sequel to *A Doll's House;* gives a terrifying warning of the consequences of holding on to the false 'idealist's dream' and refusing to meet reality. Although the linear synopses of the plays in *The Quintessence* destroy the emphasis of Ibsen's retrospective technique by which our understanding of the present action involves a growing discovery of the past shared with the characters, Shaw does demonstrate the essential dramatic movement from stereotype, presupposition and prejudice towards the climactic revelation of truth. We may well feel that the breezy clarity of his prose is no adequate vehicle for expressing the enigmatic and mysterious form which that truth takes in Ibsen. But Shaw registers the continuous and unresting nature of truth-seeking in Ibsen's work. Within each individual play, from play to play within the canon, Ibsen never allows his audience or readers to settle into the unquestioned assumption that the truth is now before them. The fallacious ideals exposed could include, for example, the apparently Ibsenian ideal of truth-telling represented by Gregers Werle in *The Wild Duck*. Shaw did not, as is sometimes supposed, reduce Ibsen's drama to problem plays with problems which could be solved once and for all by sexual equality, free love, or hygienic drains. The struggle which he saw in Ibsen between idealism and realism was to be a continuing one with no final and unequivocal victory for the latter. The appropriate response to an Ibsen play was open-ended questioning rather than confident enlightenment.

What Shaw admired in Ibsen was his seriousness as an artist, his anti-idealistic stance, and the dialectic structure of his works. In all of these Shaw may be said to have taken Ibsen as his model when he began to write plays himself. Although accusations of influence provoked Shaw into perverse disclaimers – he insisted that *Widowers' Houses* had been started years before he had even heard of Ibsen – no one is likely to miss the obvious Ibsenism of much of Shaw's early work. In fact for generations Shaw was commonly described as the English disciple of Ibsen. But in the unique and distinctive form of comedy of ideas which Shaw developed in the 1890s we must recognise an extraordinary hybrid. There could scarcely be two writers more unlike than Wilde and Ibsen, yet Shaw's plays partake of the nature of both. We could call Shaw, with as much truth as he called Wilde, 'our only thorough. playwright. He plays with everything: with wit, with philosophy, with drama, with actors and audience, with the whole theatre.' Ibsen, on the other hand, is the least playful of dramatists. If Shaw at his most Wildean yet reveals characteristics which identify him with Ibsen, at his most Ibsenian he is still not far from the comic mood and manner of Wilde.

A Pleasant and an Unpleasant play may be taken to illustrate the point. *You Never Can Tell* is undoubtedly Shaw's most Wildean play; what is more, it most closely resembles the Wilde play which Shaw professed to dislike, *The Importance of Being Earnest*. The farcical success of both depend on the skill and lightness of touch with which Shaw and Wilde create an absurd world which barely touches on the real. In the spirit of Lady Bracknell's celebrated line – 'To lose one parent, Mr Worthing, may be regarded as a misfortune; to lose both looks like carelessness' – is Valentine's benevolent advice to the fatherless Phil and Dolly:

> We dont bother much about dress and manners in England, because, as a nation, we dont dress well and weve no manners. But – and now you will excuse my frankness? [*They nod*]. Thank you. Well, in a seaside resort theres one thing you must have before anybody can afford to be seen going about with you; and thats a father, alive or dead. Am I to infer that you have omitted that indispensable part of your social equipment? (CP, I, 677)

Margery Morgan suggests that in *You Never Can Tell* Shaw gave comic expression to some of the unhappiness of his own separated family.[13] Perhaps; but more to the point is her observation that the separation and reunion of parents and children is one of the oldest of comic themes. Both Shaw and Wilde stand at the end of the long European tradition of comedy and play knowingly with its familiar conventions. The device of the foundling and the long-lost parent, so standard in Roman comedy, ends up with the absurdity of the lost-property office hero of *The Importance*. The coming together of father and daughter, so moving in *The Winter's Tale* and *Pericles*, becomes deliberate anti-climax in the meeting of Crampton and Gloria in *You Never Can Tell*. The delight of *The Importance* and *You Never Can Tell* is of an elegant and stylised unreality which inverts and parodies the norms of human experience.

It would be absurd to claim that there was much in *You Never Can Tell* to remind us directly of Ibsen. In fact Shaw mischievously portrays Mrs Clandon with her Ibsenite emancipation as already old-fashioned and suggests that the theatre is the only place left where 'her opinions would still pass as advanced'. But Shaw is true to his understanding of Ibsen in showing Gloria as a character who must reject her mother's image of her (however liberally and untraditionally conceived) in order to fulfil her own individuality. In the midst of the caricatures and distortions of farce, Shaw intended to introduce characters and situations of recognisable human reality. The scene between Valentine and Gloria at the end of the second act, he regarded as crucial to the success of the play. He was triumphant when the farce actor Allen Aynesworth, who had been so successful in *The Importance*, was, as he had predicted, unable to perform this scene convincingly.[14] It is not perhaps a very convincing scene in itself, and is one among many which might be used to illustrate Shaw's problems in handling love. But significantly what he wanted to do with it was to show the moment of emotional revelation which shatters the artificial self-images of the two characters. This is in some ways closer to the mood of Shakespearean comedy than of Ibsen, but it is consistent with Shaw's complaints against the heartless humour of *The Importance*, and it may remind us that even in a play as fantastic as *You Never Can Tell* he was committed to what he thought of as realism.

I shall be returning to *Mrs Warren's Profession* in more detail in the next chapter, but here it can be conveniently used to demonstrate what is Wildean in Shaw's most Ibsenian manner. In his 'Author's Apology' for the play, written in 1902, Shaw roundly rejected claims of influence: 'I never dreamt of Ibsen or De Maupassant, any more than a blacksmith shoeing a horse thinks of the blacksmith in the next county' (CP, I, 271). Maybe, but plays are written more distinctively than horses are shod, and the blacksmith in England worked on strikingly similar lines to the blacksmith in Norway. *Mrs Warren* is Shaw's equivalent to *Ghosts*, a deliberately shocking and provocative attack on the sacred nineteenth-century institution of sexual morality enshrined in marriage. Shaw and Ibsen exploited the then unspeakable aspects of sexuality, prostitution and venereal disease, to provide metaphors for what was wrong with their society, to illustrate the relation between hypocritical ideals and actual degradation. *Mrs Warren* moves, like *Ghosts*, from revelation to revelation, each one taking us further from the comfortable appearances of the first act. It is one of the few plays in which Shaw used Ibsen's characteristic 'strong curtains' to conclude each act. Central to *Mrs Warren* and to *Ghosts* is the misunderstanding and mutual discovery of the parent/child protagonists. The only partially closed gap between Oswald and Mrs Alving matches that between Mrs Warren and Vivie. The extent of Shaw and Ibsen's defiance of conventional attitudes is indicated by their common apparently unblinking acceptance of the possibility of incest.

And yet, and yet, and yet. The 'unpleasantness' of *Mrs Warren* is fresh air and sunshine in comparison with the horrors of *Ghosts*. Representative of the difference is the contrast between the two possibly incestuous relationships. However much Mrs Alving may overcome her squeamishness at the idea of incest, there remains something permanently repulsive in the flirtation between the sickly Oswald and his calculating half-sister. With Vivie and Frank Gardner, the revelation that they might be related only makes them 'babes in the wood in earnest'; their relation ends, as it began, in fairy-tale fantasy. Frank Gardner, above all, is the Wildean joker in *Mrs Warren*. His affectation of complete detachment from moral judgement, his precocious wit, align him with a tradition which runs from Wilde's epigrammatists to Saki's unbearable young men. Frank is an idler and proud of it, setting aside the pieties of industry or filial respect with debonair charm. His is a light-hearted immoralism of style and manner. One would not want *Mrs Warren* to be without the deft and deflating humour which he represents, but he makes it a play far from the tone and atmosphere of *Ghosts*. In being like Wilde and Ibsen simultaneously, Shaw is not the least bit like either of them.

Taking Wilde and Ibsen as alternative precedents for Shaw is not to suggest that they were the only two, or even necessarily the major two, influences on his work. When it comes to establishing sources of influence on Shaw, the critic is likely to suffer from an embarrassment of riches. But his attitude to Wilde and Ibsen may stand for co-ordinates within which his comedy of ideas was developed. Looking at his work in this light may help to explain why, as a playwright, he has suffered from two, apparently incompatible, forms of negative criticism. To some he has seemed the incorrigible clown whose work, amusing and brilliant as it may be, does not finally take itself seriously, the most distinguished example being Tolstoy who found Shaw's levity painful.[15] And yet equally persistent, if not more so, has been the myth of Shaw the preacher rather than the playwright, the writer whose plays were ruined by his intolerable didacticism. But Shaw's attempt to combine the Wildean tradition of manners with the purposefulness of Ibsen's realism is significant not only as it left him open to two forms of misconstruction. It was, I believe, the source of genuine and fundamental problems in his work. It led to certain crucial ambiguities in Shaw's attitude towards the drama and in the tone and substance of the plays themselves.

One example is his use of the high dramatic climax. Shaw refused to take seriously the stock situations of nineteenth-century theatre. More than one critic has ably demonstrated how he used them only to expose them, to turn them on their heads, or to reveal them in a completely new light. Even Ibsen was not exempt from Shaw's reproaches for staginess. In his obituary article in 1906, he denied that Ibsen's theatrical technique was distinctively modern: rather 'Ibsen seems to have succumbed without a struggle to the old notion that a play is not really a play unless it contains a murder, a suicide, or something else out of the Police Gazette'.[16] He stigmatised the use of such events, specifically the death of children, as 'dishonorable . . . artistic devices because they depend on a morbid horror of death and a morbid enjoyment of horror'. He adds that in the final deaths of *John Gabriel Borkman* or *When We Dead Awaken* the symbolism barely conceals 'the old conventional mortuary ending'. Yet, as Shaw concedes, 'Ibsen turns the Chamber of Horrors to astonishing and illuminating account'. Although we may well agree that the Ibsenian climaxes and catastrophes are stagey and melodramatic, he turns them into a genuine tragic vision by the sheer depth and force of his imagination. He takes them so seriously that he dares his audience to disbelieve in them; as Shaw acutely pointed out, he challenges us to say, with Judge Brack, 'people don't do such things'. But Shaw's instincts of the comedian will never allow him wholly to convince us or himself of the truth of high dramatics. As a result a scene such as the discovery of the murder of Ftatateeta in *Caesar and Cleopatra* seems like a piece of fake sensationalism in a way that Ibsen's stage deaths never do.

More basically the tension within Shaw between the Wildean comedian and the Ibsenian realist sets up difficulties for an audience as to the form of willing suspension of disbelief they are supposed to adopt towards the plays. The comic writer encourages the agreement of a viewpoint for the duration of his comedy which, though often traditional, is not necessarily to be identified with his audience's normal social attitude.[17] The viewpoint may be politically progressive or reactionary, it may be indulgent or satirically censorious, but it bears an oblique and avowedly distorted relation to the reality we know outside the theatre. Comedy contains its own form of truth, which yet cannot be applied directly as truth within an extra-theatrical world. Both the form and effect of comedy are static rather than kinetic; our lives may be enriched but not normally changed by the encounter with great comedy. In this sense a play such as *The Importance of Being Earnest*, though without anything like the depth of the greatest comedy, is true to the tradition of comic form and meaning.

It was Shaw's ambition to harness the energies of comedy, to put them to dynamic use. This was not merely a matter of combining the enjoyment of laughter with a moral, social, or political purpose – a traditional objective of the comedian, in theory at least. His aim was to move forward both his characters and his audience, to bring them to a measurably more advanced stage of self-understanding. His Ibsenian dialectic committed him to a progressive view of truth itself, and in that view comedy had its part to play. By his teasing and his clowning, Shaw believed he could help to make his audience more fully aware of their real situation. But it was not merely obtuseness on the part of the public which so often defeated this purpose in the plays. If they laughed and ignored the message, or objected to the message as preachiness, it was partly because the status of reality in the plays was equivocal, the special distorted vision of the comic fighting the claim to absolute or realistic truth.

2 Pleasant/Unpleasant

With the publication of *Plays: Pleasant and Unpleasant* in 1898, Shaw staked his claim to be regarded as a significant dramatist. He contrives to suggest in the Prefaces to the two volumes that his career as a playwright was accidental, begun out of a determination to 'manufacture the evidence' in the case for the New Drama in England, and continued out of habit. He paints an amusing picture of himself as an ageing and tiring journalist driven to the expedient of collecting his ephemera – 'I will begin with small sins: I will publish my plays' (CP, I, 16). And yet as always with Shaw, the self-puncturing buffoonery is combined with the attitude of self-advertising conceit. He does not blame the theatre managers for refusing to perform his plays – by 1898 he had still not had a major professional production in England; but he blames the con-temporary theatre itself, the tastes of the theatre-going public, and the training of the actors for making his plays unplayable. It is not, he insists, the fastidious contempt of the literary man for the theatre which drives him to publication. In preparing the texts, he claims, 'I have tried to put down nothing that is irrelevant to the actor's performance, and, through it, to the audience's comprehension of the play' (CP, I, 32). It is rather in despair at finding actors, directors or audience sufficiently skilled and intelligent to interpret or appreciate his plays, that he resorts to displaying them in his own way.

Much of this is stock Shavianism – a continuation of his drama critic's crusade against the shortcomings of 'our theatres in the nineties'. But the Prefaces to *Plays: Pleasant and Unpleasant* do significantly articulate Shaw's strategy as a dramatist, and the antithesis pleasant/unpleasant itself is of importance in defining their effect. Indirectly the title suggests a challenge to the traditional division, tragedy/comedy. Although the subject matter of the Unpleasant plays is 'the crimes of society' and that of the Pleasant plays 'its romantic follies', corresponding to the neo-classical dictum that comedy should 'sport with human follies not with crimes', both

14

categories have a common purpose cutting across the generic division:

> To me the tragedy and comedy of life lie in the consequences, sometimes terrible, sometimes ludicrous, of our persistent attempts to found our institutions on the ideals suggested to our imaginations by our half-satisfied passions, instead of on a genuinely scientific natural history. (CP, 1, 385)

It is such 'a genuinely scientific natural history' that Shaw claims he has given us in *Plays: Pleasant and Unpleasant*.

'I created nothing; I invented nothing; I imagined nothing; I perverted nothing; I simply discovered drama in real life' (CP, 1, 508). This was Shaw's defence as a 'dramatic realist to his critics' against charges of extravagance, moral perversity, or whimsical distortion. It is remarkable how early he had conceived this 'realistic' tactic. In a letter to the publisher Macmillan in 1880, he explained the object of his first novel *Immaturity*:

> to write a novel scrupulously true to nature, with no incident in it to which everyday experience might not afford a parallel, and yet which should constantly provoke in [a] reader full of the emotional ethics of the conventional novel, a sense of oddity and unexpectedness. (CL, 1, 27)

Such is his aim throughout *Plays: Pleasant and Unpleasant*: in the Unpleasant volume 'to force the spectator to face unpleasant facts'; in the Pleasant plays, to laugh his audience good-humouredly out of their romantic illusions. In both cases reality is where we are to come out.

And yet is it where we do come out? Our expectations are no longer those of the late nineteenth-century readers and audiences for whom the realistic technique was designed, and yet do we not feel much of that same sense of oddity and alienation expressed by Shaw's first critics? We might perhaps expect the plays to have dated badly as the Victorian complacencies they assailed are not our complacencies and the unpleasant facts they reveal have little or no shock value; yet they have dated surprisingly little and even as topical a play as *The Philanderer* can hold a modern audience.[1] If Shaw's strategy does not work as he apparently intended it should, it is not because the reality which it aimed to expose is now

commonplace. It is rather that we have doubts about whether what
Shaw gives us finally *is* emotional or imaginative reality. I want in
this chapter to look at two of the Unpleasant plays, *Widowers' Houses*
and *Mrs Warren's Profession*, and two of the Pleasant, *Arms and the
Man* and *Candida*, to consider what is the effect in practice of Shaw's
theory of dramatic realism.

From a Victorian point of view, the basic subject matter of the
Unpleasant plays made them unpleasant. All three are concerned
more or less with sex and social economics and, most originally and
improbably, with the relation between the two. *Widowers' Houses*, at
first sight, might appear to be all social economics and very little sex.
Its object clearly is to take its audience with the naive hero, Harry
Trench, from ignorance and naiveté through disillusionment to a
recognition of complicity with Sartorius, the rack-renting slum-
landlord. As Shaw says at the end of the Unpleasant Preface: 'I must
warn my readers that my attacks are directed against themselves,
not against my stage figures' (CP, I, 34). It is in fact one of Shaw's
most forceful and lucid polemic demonstrations of the capitalist
system. The simple shock of Harry Trench at Sartorius's arguments
which prove him a sleeping partner in the business he has just
indignantly spurned makes for a very effective dramatic moment.
He is, as Shaw's stage direction puts it, 'morally beggared'.
However, Shaw goes beyond this revelation of one of the least
acceptable faces of capitalism. He shows the more acceptable, but
no less dishonest, face which is turned towards the public at a
slightly later stage of the development of the capitalist society.
However improbable it may be that Lickcheese, the penurious rent-
collector of Act II, should be transformed into the prosperous
entrepreneur of Act III, he is used to show the slum-landlord how to
change his colours in an atmosphere of changed public opinion.
Sartorius will appear to become a model property-owner but only to
win compensation from the city authorities when his property is
requisitioned for the building of a new road. Plain rack-renting
gives way to more complicated forms of municipal swindling: the
capitalist continues to accumulate capital.

The love-plot between Trench and Blanche may appear to be not
much more than a peg on which to hang all of the economic
analysis, the relic of William Archer's 'well-made' plot with which
Widowers' House started. It gave Shaw the conventional structure for
comedy: Act I, exposition, boy meets girl; Act II, complication, boy

loses girl; Act III, dénouement, boy gets girl after all. In the first
edition of the play, published in 1893 as the initial volume in the
short-lived Independent Theatre series, the romantic plot is little
more than that, set in ironic counterpoint to the pattern of social
analysis. Trench and Blanche's reunion at the end represents his
final acceptance of the status quo and his part in it. The dialogue
between the two in the original text stands out as particularly stagey
and inept; Shaw at that stage was trying unsuccessfully to parody
stock scenes of lovers' comic vagaries. In the revised text of 1898, the
dialogue is strikingly tightened up and given point and emphasis by
Shavian stage direction. Anyone who is inclined to think of Shaw's
stage directions as prosy and untheatrical should see how sensitively
and incisively he orchestrates the dramatic movement of the scene
between Blanche and Trench in the second act in comparison with
the straight dialogue of the original text.[2]

However the 1898 revision of the play was not merely a matter of
bringing the Blanche/Trench relationship into better focus. It
involved a basic re-thinking of the character of Blanche and an
attempt to deepen the psychological underpinning of the play. In
1893 Blanche had been fairly conventionally missish, although she
was already given the spectacular display of temper when she pulls
the parlourmaid's hair. Shaw seemed at that stage to waver between
coquette and termagant in his characterisation. In the 1898 revision
he tried to integrate the two roles into a consistent psychology.
Blanche is made much more dominant in the relationship with
Trench from the start, forthright and direct in their first interview
instead of indulging in elaborate lovers' charades. Most remarkably, the scene with the parlourmaid is given a quite new slant.
In the original version it was no more than a crude illustration of the
brutality of the so-called lady with her inferiors; Annie, as she was
then named, was a stock parlourmaid, annoyed at being inter-
rupted at her work, accustomed to putting up with the violence of
her mistress. But in 1898 she becomes 'a snivelling, sympathetic
creature' who looks at Blanche with 'abject wounded affection and
bodily terror'. Shaw's object is not increased pathos but an almost
open suggestion of sado-sexuality:

> The Parlormaid [*plaintively*]: You speak so brutal to me, Miss
> Blanche; and I do love you so. I'm sure no one else would stay
> and put up with what I have to put up with.

Blanche: Then go. I dont want you. Do you hear. Go.
The Parlormaid [*piteously, falling on her knees*]: Oh no, Miss Blanche.
  Dont send me away from you: dont —
Blanche [*with fierce disgust*]: Agh! I hate the sight of you. [*The maid,
  wounded to the heart, cries bitterly*]. (CP, I, 97)[3]

In its revised form, the scene ties in with the final meeting and
reconciliation with Trench which Shaw introduces in the 1898 text
with very explicit stage directions:

For a moment they stand face to face, quite close to one another,
she provocative, taunting, half defying, half inviting him to
advance, in a flush of undisguised animal excitement. It suddenly
flashes on him that all this ferocity is erotic: that she is making love
to him. His eye lights up: a cunning expression comes into the
corners of his mouth: with a heavy assumption of indifference he
walks straight back to his chair, and plants himself in it with his
arms folded. (CP, I, 119)

Trench triumphs finally in the battle of the sexes by refusing to
respond to her attempted humiliation of him, by his silence
reducing her to tenderness. The climax of this catch-as-catch-can
relationship then snaps into place as the marriage which clinches
the shady deal to be engineered by Sartorius and Lickcheese, and
thus completes Trench's assimilation into the corrupt capitalist
world. Shaw was trying to go beyond merely showing the inter-
dependence of love and marriage with an economic social system.
He was suggesting an aggressiveness and rapacity in the sexual life
of his middle-class characters which matched the reality of their
money-making.

Shaw, however, was no Strindberg, much less a Genet. He did
not find the joy of life 'in life's cruel and mighty conflicts'.[4] The
scene between Blanche and the parlourmaid, the sexual ferocity of
the final meeting with Trench, are out of key with the sour social
comedy which makes up the rest of the play. Much has been made of
the peculiarities of Shaw's own sexual life – or the lack of it – by
critics from Frank Harris on.[5] But whatever the biographical or
psychological explanation, sexuality was to remain an area of
difficulty for him on the stage. In *The Philanderer* he tried to explore
further links between sexual and social relationships, and to show
that the 'womanly woman' and the 'manly man' were slaves to
passion as well as slaves to institutional custom and convention. But

the play remains acutely uncomfortable and uncertain in its moral and emotional attitudes. At times Shaw seems to be inviting us to identify with the smug self-satisfaction of Charteris, disengaging himself from the possessive clasp of Julia Craven. At times it seems rather that the play is an act of guilty remorse, expiating a sense of wrong done to Julia's original.[6] More than anything else one detects in Shaw a desire 'to quit such odious subjects'. There may be an element of wishful thinking in his imagination of 'a drama in which love should be as effectively ignored as cholera is at present' (CP, I, 240). Placing it on a level with a contagious disease is not merely Shavian paradox. In both *Widowers' Houses* and *The Philanderer* sex itself seems to be as tainted as society is, and to stand in as much need of radical alteration. Failing the possibility of such alteration, Shaw's implication seems to be that we should give it up altogether.

There is a case for calling *Widowers' Houses* the most unpleasant play Shaw ever wrote. 'Nobody', said Shaw in the Preface to the first edition, 'will find it a beautiful or lovable work'.

> It is saturated with the vulgarity of the life it represents: the people do not speak nobly, live gracefully, or sincerely face their own position: the author is not giving expression in pleasant fancies to the underlying beauty and romance of happy life, but dragging up to the smooth surface of 'respectability' a handful of the slime and foulness of its polluted bed, and playing off your laughter at the scandal of the exposure against your shudder at its blackness. (CP, I, 45)

For all its rhetoric, Shaw makes good this claim in *Widowers' Houses*. The play *is* 'saturated with the vulgarity of the life it represents'; it has not a single character inviting admiration or sympathy. Though Sartorius is given some eloquence in the vein to be exploited afterwards by Mrs Warren and Andrew Undershaft, he has all the bullying insecurity of the self-made man without the real dignity of the later Shavian devil's advocates. The stock stage confidant Cokane is made into a disgusting sort of hanger-on, supplying bits and bobs of suave euphemism to cover the unsavoury facts of any situation. Shaw makes a very good case for his Unpleasant play in his Preface:

> My life has been passed mostly in big modern towns, where my sense of beauty has been starved whilst my intellect has been

gorged with problems like that of the slums in this play, until at last I have come, in a horrible sort of way, to relish them enough to make them the subjects of my essays as an artist. (CP, I, 45)

Yet Shaw had less relish for unpleasantness than he here makes out, and though all his life he delighted in shocking his audiences by the unexpectedness of his subjects or their treatment, he did not enjoy arousing pain or disgust. It is no accident that he moved from Unpleasant to Pleasant plays, nor yet that *Mrs Warren's Profession*, supposedly the most unpleasant of the lot, is much less repulsive than *Widowers' Houses*.

It is curious that it should be so, because Shaw adopts very much the same strategy in *Mrs Warren* as in his first Unpleasant play, and in many ways makes it still more powerful. Vivie Warren takes the place of Harry Trench as the young person to be disillusioned and educated in the economic ways of the world. She, like Trench, is forced to see that there is no moral barrier between herself and the debauched capitalist, Sir George Crofts, whom she despises. Her line of appalled discovery to Crofts is Trench's line to Sartorius – 'I believe I am just as bad as you'. The point is made all the more powerfully in *Mrs Warren* as Shaw is using a more devastating metaphor for his diagnosis of the malaise of his society. The working-man may have nothing to sell but his labour; the working woman has nothing to sell but herself. 'The only way for a woman to provide for herself decently is for her to be good to some man that can afford to be good to her' (CP, I, 314). Shaw's indictment is a far-reaching one. He is not only attacking the level of women's wages which forces them to prostitution, but he is making the equation between disreputable prostitution and its respectable counterpart in marriage with a similar economic dependence of women on men. Beyond that again, he is arguing polemically that the normal activity of capitalism is prostitution, the money-making exploitation of human bodies or human talents:

we not only condemn women as a sex to attach themselves to breadwinners, licitly or illicitly, on pain of heavy privation and disadvantage; but we have great prostitute classes of men: for instance, the playwrights and journalists, to whom I myself belong, not to mention the legions of lawyers, doctors, clergymen, and platform politicians who are daily using their highest faculties to belie their real sentiments. (CP, I, 33–4)

Whether or not we agree with this analysis, it is cogently and dramatically argued in *Mrs Warren*. What gives the play more depth and more interest than *Widowers' Houses*, however, is the relationship between Vivie and her mother which is its emotional dynamic. Shaw was developing here what was only a hint in a scene between Blanche and Sartorius. When Sartorius realises how completely his daughter despises the working-classes from which her father came, he comments '[*coldly and a little wistfully*] I see I have made a real lady of you, Blanche' (CP, I, 110). Similarly in *Mrs Warren*, the gap between Mrs Warren and Vivie is a gap she has created. 'I was a good mother; and because I made my daughter a good woman she turns me out as if I was a leper' (CP, I, 355). Where it is only a passing observation in *Widowers' Houses*, Shaw gives his full attention in *Mrs Warren* to the effect on human relationships of the upward drive in a class-conscious society.

The most striking difference between the two plays which makes *Mrs Warren* so much more characteristically Shavian is that the majority of its characters are likeable. Blanche's passionate distaste for those beneath her – 'I hate the poor' – is presented as the ugly truth of her character; though we feel some sympathy for Sartorius in having created this lady-like monster, we feel more that the punishment fits the crime. In *Mrs Warren*, as in so many of Shaw's plays, we are asked to sympathise equally with Vivie and her mother, to engage emotionally with both their attitudes, and some measure of such sympathy is extended to all the other characters as well. Praed, occupying a similar supernumerary position to that of Cokane in *Widowers' Houses*, is as aimlessly pleasant as Cokane is aimlessly obnoxious. Frank Gardner adds a lightness and witty grace to the play which Shaw sternly excluded from *Widowers' Houses*.[7] His father is a mere laughing-stock. Only Sir George Crofts is a pure villain, possibly the first and last pure villain in Shaw's dramatic work.

The genial tolerance, the general sympathy towards his characters could be seen as evidence of Shaw's fair-mindedness, his comprehensive creative understanding. But it also makes for a degree of cosiness in his work. We may well feel that he likes most of his characters and can make them likeable to us; we may laugh at their stupidity but at worst they are harmless. There is frequently here, however, no more than a fairly shallow sort of good will, very far – to take a supreme example – from the imaginative sympathies of Tolstoy who can make us understand a Dolokhov as deeply as a

Natasha. It would, of course, be preposterous to use Tolstoy as a
stick to beat Shaw. Tolstoy is a psychological novelist, Shaw is a
comedian; the comparison is by definition inappropriate. Yet there
is in Shaw a reluctance to look into the more sinister quality of
human beings which should be acknowledged and not confused
with the imaginative charity of the greatest writers. We are close to
tragedy at moments in *Mrs Warren*, but Shaw pulls us back because
he refuses to allow himself to believe in a tragic sense of things.

Vivie takes the place of Harry Trench in *Widowers' Houses* as the
innocent to be educated, but Shaw is far more interested in her than
he was in Trench. In her, he claimed he

> put on the stage for the first time . . . the highly educated,
> capable, independent young woman of the governing class as we
> know her today, working, smoking, preferring the society of men
> to that of women simply because men talk about the questions
> that interest her and not about servants & babies, making no
> pretence of caring much about art or romance, respectable
> through sheer usefulness & strength, and playing the part of the
> charming woman only as the amusement of her life, not as its
> serious occupation. (CL, I, 566–7)

Shaw's admiration rings out from every line of this. He takes delight
in the horror of the aesthete Praed confronted by Vivie's matter-of-
fact creed: 'I like working and getting paid for it. When I'm tired of
working, I like a comfortable chair, a cigar, a little whiskey, and a
novel with a good detective story in it' (CP, I, 278). This is
caricature of course, and Shaw makes Frank Gardner spot it as such
with his comment on Vivie's cigar-smoking – 'Nasty womanly
habit. Nice men dont do it any longer' (CP, I, 336). But all the same,
Vivie's no-nonsense efficiency, her intolerance of shibboleths and
sentimentality, mark her for Shavian approval through most of
the first and second acts.

This makes the turn-around of the major scene between Vivie
and her mother which occupies the last half of Act II all the more
remarkable. There is no question of the sort of walk-over here which
Sartorius achieved with Trench. Vivie seems set to win and win
easily in her battle with Mrs Warren, coolly unimpressed as she is by
maternal rhetoric. Shaw signals the turn in the tide in two crucial
stage directions:

Mrs Warren: You! youve no heart. [*She suddenly breaks out vehemently in her natural tongue – the dialect of a woman of the people – with all her affectations of maternal authority and conventional manners gone, and an overwhelming inspiration of true conviction and scorn in her*] Oh, I wont bear it: I wont put up with the injustice of it. What right have you to set yourself up above me like this? You boast of what you are to me – to me, who gave you the chance of being what you are. What chance had I! Shame on you for a bad daughter and a stuck-up prude!

Vivie[*sitting down with a shrug, no longer confident; for her replies, which have sounded sensible and strong to her so far, now begin to ring rather woodenly and even priggishly against the new tone of her mother*]: Dont think for a moment I set myself above you in any way. (CP, I, 309)

Mrs Warren's revelation of her past life which follows, carrying with it Shaw's polemic anti-capitalist argument, knocks us backward by its emotional force, as it does Vivie. It is hard not to echo Vivie's exclamation:

[*fascinated, gazing at her*] My dear mother: you are a wonderful woman: you are stronger than all England. And are you really and truly not one wee bit doubtful – or – or – ashamed? (CP, I, 315)

The scene works so powerfully because it represents a wholly unexpected explosion of feeling for which we, like Vivie, are unprepared and which shatters the complacency of our earlier attitude.

But this is only the first stage in Vivie's moral education. The woman who took to prostitution rather than accept the economic slavery of 'respectable' working-class life Vivie could respect, admire, even love as her mother. But the current managing directress of an international chain of brothels in Brussels, Vienna, Ostend and Budapest is a different matter. Sir George Crofts' revelation leaves Vivie feeling not merely 'morally beggared', but appallingly polluted. 'Damn you', shouts Crofts at the height of his conventional villain's rage.

Vivie: You need not. I feel among the damned already. (CP, I, 332)

The melodrama at the end of this scene with Crofts' parting-shot –
the suggestion that Vivie and Frank are siblings – and the business
with the rifle, are not quite convincingly handled. Revisions in the
manuscript draft of the play demonstrate Shaw's uncertainty here.[8]
But Vivie's reaction of horror when Frank tries to play their old
love-games is credible enough in the circumstances. As she makes
clear, it is not the idea of incest that revolts her, but everything to do
with sex is tainted in her mind.[9]

Shaw took pride in the fact that the consequences of his play's
dramatic revelation 'though cruel enough, are all quite sensible &
sober, no suicide or sensational tragedy of any sort' (CL, 1, 566).
Instead therefore of allowing Vivie to use Frank's rifle on herself, she
is made to flee to 'Honoria Fraser's chambers, 67 Chancery Lane,
for the rest of my life' (CP, 1, 334). It would make sense to interpret
this as the act of someone emotionally maimed, determined to
escape from the horror of self-analysis and the vulnerability of
relationship. The Vivie that we see in the fourth act has features that
might be played that way. She can still not bring herself to name her
mother's trade. What is for Praed the romantic suggestiveness of
Europe – 'the gaiety, the vivacity, the happy air of Brussels' – can
only be a horrific reminder to Vivie of what she wants to forget. But
Shaw refuses to allow us to see Vivie's deliberate stripping of herself
of attachments, friend, lover, mother, in negative terms. A life-time
of actuarial accountancy is not to be viewed as a self-denying
cloister. The burden of the first act was that this is what a modern
young woman actually wants, and that therefore in the final act
Vivie is merely going about her business. We are supposed once
again to admire her lack of conventional womanliness and her
dedication to purposeful activity.

This all makes for ambiguity in the final scene with Mrs Warren,
which is intended to match the earlier interview in Act II. This time
we get just what we expected then – a victory for the cool rationalist
over the mother who tries alternately to bully and wheedle. 'I wish
you wouldn't rant, mother. It only hardens me.' Vivie dismisses Mrs
Warren with a final and considered verdict: 'If I had been you,
mother, I might have done as you did; but I should not have lived
one life and believed in another. You are a conventional woman at
heart. That is why I am bidding you goodbye now' (CP, 1, 355).
Shaw apparently intends us to go along with this. Yet it is hard to
avoid feeling that the tone here is much the same wooden
priggishness of which Vivie stood convicted in Act II. At least the

emotional relationship which that earlier scene opened up should .not be closed with such a definitive snapping shut of the ledger.

Mrs Warren leaves and Vivie is left alone to her work. Critical views differ as to what the final effect of the play's ending is. For Eric Bentley it represents an unmitigated triumph for Vivie: 'The events and discoveries of the play are her education . . . and for the first of many times in Shavian drama the core and culmination of the play is a personal crisis, a disillusionment, almost a conversion. A soul is born.'[10] This is to make Vivie a prototype for Major Barbara, her work in the accounting office an analogue to Barbara's 'return to the colours'. Charles Carpenter is more doubtful:

> Vivie's final actions convey an almost palpable sense of wasted vitality. After her dismissals of Praed, Frank and Mrs Warren . . . her vigorous plunge into actuarial calculations leaves a marked residue of frustration. Two feelings are evoked: admiration for her energy and distaste for its specific application.[11]

It is not at all clear that Shaw would have shared that distaste and it may well be that he intended the scene to be interpreted as the happy ending which Bentley claims. But if so, then we are entitled to feel cheated by the play. There are tragic implications in the scenes between Vivie and her mother which Shaw refuses to see through to the end. The emotional anti-climax of their final meeting is not merely a matter of refusing to give the audience the high dramatics they expect. It shirks the possibility of permanent damage to Vivie, permanent loss to Mrs Warren as the outcome of their relationship. And in this the play, for all the audacity of its attack on orthodox social attitudes, lets its audience off the hook.

For Shaw any experience, however painful, could be turned to profit. Disillusionment was always enlightenment for him – a step towards greater understanding. That is why he refuses to take Vivie's tragedy tragically and prefers to represent her using the pain of her discovery of the truth about her mother as the momentum for a new life. Human beings that could not be educated by their errors were, as far as Shaw was concerned, morally useless. In so far as he came to recognise a tragic predicament in human life it was only in the shortness of the learning process; given time enough – the three hundred years of *Back to Methusaleh* – people would grow up. And for the same reason that Shaw denied the irredeemable suffering of tragedy, he was not really interested in the irremediable characters of comedy. Most of the standard comic figures, with their *idées fixes* and their monomanias, are by definition incapable of change or development. Shaw could use such comic types to brilliant effect, but they were never central and they were always supposed to be subordinated to the characters whose progress forward was the mainspring of the play.

Sergius in *Arms and the Man* is a striking case in point. Sergius's Byronism is intended to be a much more important comic object-lesson than the vaguer Romanticism which afflicts the other characters. Shaw describes him at length in an introductory stage-direction.

> By his brooding on the perpetual failure, not only of others, but of himself, to live up to his ideals; by his consequent cynical scorn for humanity; by his jejeune credulity as to the absolute validity of his concepts and the unworthiness of the world in disregarding them; by his wincings and mockeries under the sting of the petty disillusions which every hour spent among men brings to his sensitive observation, he has acquired the half tragic, half ironic air, the mysterious moodiness, the suggestion of a strange and terrible history that has left nothing but undying remorse, by which Childe Harold fascinated the grandmothers of his English contemporaries. (CP, I, 419)

It is not merely Sergius's idealism which Shaw mocks – 'his jejeune credulity as to the absolute validity of his concepts' – it is the equally childish cynicism which goes with it. Cynicism was the charge most frequently brought against Shaw himself, and most hotly denied. For him the cynic was a disillusioned romantic who misapplied the lesson of his disillusion, despising reality rather than recognising the foolishness of the ideal against which he set it. Sergius with his 'I never apologise, I never withdraw' is a comic delight; as Shaw himself was quick to point out, his is *the* star comic part in the play. But the very fixity of the attitudes, the temperamental impossibility of his escaping from the idealism/cynicism cycle, mark him down as beyond Shavian redemption.

Freud divides jokes into the innocent and the tendentious. In his own special sense of the word, Shaw would have claimed that all of his jokes were tendentious, none of them innocent. The 'tendency' of *Arms and the Man* was to deflate romantic illusions about war and replace them with the reality. But on closer inspection, many of

Shaw's tendentious jokes turn out to be innocent after all. 'I am quite aware', Shaw proclaims with pride,

> that the much criticised Swiss officer in Arms and The Man is not a conventional stage soldier. He suffers from want of food and sleep; his nerves go to pieces after three days under fire, ending in the horrors of a rout and pursuit; he has found by experience that it is more important to have a few bits of chocolate to eat in the field than cartridges for his revolver. When many of my critics rejected these circumstances as fantastically improbable and cynically unnatural, it was not necessary to argue them into common sense: all I had to do was to brain them, so to speak, with the first half dozen military authorities at hand, beginning with the present Commander in Chief. (CP, I, 383–4)

'Brained' they may have been, but it is unlikely that any of Shaw's critics were convinced that Bluntschli was a life-like soldier by the military authorities cited. Bluntschli is as much a creature of fantasy as Sergius, and the real comic joy of *Arms and the Man* derives from the collision of one form of fantasy with another.

From the beginning of the play, its art is the art of anti-climax. We are prepared for melodrama with the entrance of the stranger into Raina's bedroom and the character of the matter-of-fact Bluntschli is a calculated let-down. We laugh at ourselves for having been scared in the scene where Raina is threatened with the pistol when it is revealed that the pistol was not loaded, and still more when Bluntschli confesses that he always carries chocolate rather than ammunition in any case. No doubt Shaw is right that, especially for an artillery officer, pistols would be of little value in battle, but the episode of the chocolate-creams hardly produces the effect of verisimilitude. We are relieved and delighted by the absurdity of it, because it assures us that we are safely in a comic world where bullets are replaced with chocolate-creams. It is of course all too true that soldiers' nerves suffer under prolonged bombardment; but when Bluntschli tells Raina that all she need to do make him cry 'is to scold me as if I were a little boy and you my nurse', we are far from the horrors of shell-shock.

The main set-piece of Shaw's debunking in the first act is Sergius's cavalry charge. For Raina and Catherine, in the brief first scene, it was the fulfilment of all their heroic dreams. Bluntschli's professional view of it is beautifully calculated to deglamourise.

Raina [*eagerly turning to him, as all her enthusiasm and her dreams of glory rush back on her*]: Did you see the great cavalry charge? Oh, tell me about it. Describe it to me.

The Man: You never saw a cavalry charge, did you?

Raina: How could I?

The Man: Ah, perhaps not. No: of course not! Well it's a funny sight. It's like slinging a handful of peas against a window pane: first one comes; then two or three close behind him; and then all the rest in a lump.

Raina [*her eyes dilating as she raises her clasped hands ecstatically*]: Yes, first One! the bravest of the brave!

The Man [*prosaically*]: Hm! you should see the poor devil pulling at his horse.

Raina: Why should he pull at his horse?

The Man [*impatient of so stupid a question*]: It's running away with him, of course: do you suppose the fellow wants to get there before the others and be killed? (CP, I, 403)

Once again Shaw was in a position to defend this as a truer representation of the reality of a cavalry charge than Raina's romantic ideal, and even produced accounts of the Charge of the Light Brigade to prove it. But the spirit of a passage like this is one of mischievous iconoclasm rather than realism. We laugh at the pure incongruity of Raina's ecstatic 'first One! the bravest of the brave' punctured by Bluntschli's 'you should have seen the poor devil pulling at his horse'. The image of 'slinging a handful of peas against a window pane' is a comic meiosis, a ridiculous cutting down to size of the heroic associations of the cavalry charge. But once again, as with the chocolate-creams, it affords the reassurance of harmlessness typical of comedy.

There is one speech, and one speech only, in *Arms and the Man* which brings home the grim reality of war. In the midst of the thickest of the comic confusion between Sergius, Raina and Bluntschli in Act III it is revealed that Bluntschli's friend who had passed on the story of his midnight escapade at the Petkoffs' is 'dead. Burnt alive'.

Bluntschli: Shot in the hip in a woodyard. Couldn't drag himself out. Your fellows' shells set the timber on fire and burnt him, with half a dozen other poor devils in the same predicament. (CP, I, 458–9)

Shaw sternly rebuked his first audiences for laughing at this, but it was in part his own fault. In the atmosphere of hilarity raised by the lovers' quarrels, it is hard to adjust to this one horribly sober reminder of the background of war. Everywhere else in the play romantic ideals of war are debunked, but not replaced by reality, at least not with the reality of violence and death. Shaw no doubt chose to make his protagonist a Swiss mercenary because the Swiss (with the lone exception of William Tell) are the European nation least associated with military heroism, and the mercenary is a professional soldier without the conventional afflatus of patriotism. Bluntschli's experienced soldiership comes out most strongly in his capacity for logistics – the mundane and necessary work which the amateurs, Sergius and Petkoff, find impossible. Margery Morgan is surely right to identify *Arms and the Man* as a 'tale for the nursery', with Bluntschli the grown-up among the overgrown children who make up the rest of the cast.[12] He represents a guarantee against unpleasantness for us in the audience as well as for the characters on the stage.

Arms and the Man is a Pleasant play; it would be ridiculous to complain that it does not do justice to the horrors of war. It would seem unnecessary indeed, to demonstrate the self-evidently fantastic nature of its comedy, if it were not for Shaw's claim to the status of dramatic realist. It is not only that he was prepared to defend the actions of his characters as life-like on the evidence of his military authorities. But in *Arms and the Man*, as in all his plays, we are supposed to learn and develop with the central characters, for all the fantastic atmosphere. Two moments in particular stand out as crucial to Shaw's educative strategy. The first is Bluntschli's reference to himself as 'a man who has spoiled all his chances in life through an incurably romantic disposition' (CP, I, 468). Shaw intends his audience to react to this as Sergius does, with 'incredulous amazement'. But Bluntschli makes good the statement:

> I ran away from home twice when I was a boy. I went into the army instead of into my father's business. I climbed the balcony of this house when a man of sense would have dived into the nearest cellar. I came sneaking back here to have another look at the young lady when any other man of my age would have sent the coat back . . . and gone quietly home. (CP, I, 468)

Yet if Bluntschli here turns the tables on our judgement of him as the anti-romantic, he is to be undercut next when he reveals that he has taken the twenty-three-year-old Raina for seventeen.

Shaw's object in both moves, we may guess, is to afford a new perspective on the relationship between Bluntschli and Raina, and force us to take their marriage at least partly seriously. Bluntschli's real romanticism, as distinct from Sergius's pose, is his restlessness, his willingness to follow instinct and impulse. In this he is presumably one of the first of Shaw's heroes of the Life Force. Equally, for all her posing, we are intended to see in Raina's feeling for her 'chocolate-cream soldier' something more than a schoolgirl crush, which was in fact all her love for Sergius was. But none of this seems convincing in context. Instead we feel that Shaw has merely pulled another couple of rabbits out of his comedian's hat. On the whole the ending of *Arms and the Man* is marvellously well handled – the inventory of Bluntschli's hotels as the evidence of his eligibility for Raina's hand is a stroke of comic genius. But the attempt to suggest that there is any form of emotional reality underlying it is likely to be quite properly ignored by an audience. *Arms and the Man* has just that superficial degree of resemblance to reality which is necessary for the best fantastic comedy. Any claim that it has more would destroy our appreciation of its peculiar excellence.

In July 1894 Shaw defended *Arms and the Man* as 'A Dramatic Realist to his Critics'. But some months earlier, he had denied that he was 'an advocate for stage realism': 'I am an advocate for stage illusion; stage realism is a contradiction in terms. I am only a realist in a Platonic sense' (CP, I, 483) This is quite an important statement, for all its air of Shavian perversity. Shaw was not interested in reality for reality's sake on the stage, the painstaking naturalism of Antoine, for instance. When he claims to be an advocate for stage illusion, he means the artful illusion of reality which it was the object of all great acting to produce, by whatever method, realistic or romantic. The statement that he is 'a realist in a Platonic sense' goes deeper still. Shaw is here hinting that his ultimate interest is not in the reality of the here and now but in a transcendental reality equivalent to Plato's world of the forms. His tactic, like Plato's, is to subvert preconceptions and conventional judgements in a continuing dialectic of truth-seeking. Shaw gives warning here that his realism may involve an apparent rejection of the actual for the visionary.

It is consistent with this attitude that Shaw should have followed *Arms and the Man* with *Candida*. In *Arms and the Man* the idealist

Sergius had been shown up by the down-to-earth Bluntschli. In *Candida* it is the turn of the practical Morell to be the butt, and the romantic poet Marchbanks the hero. This is not merely a matter of Shaw avoiding type-casting, showing that he could make as good a case against pragmatism as for it. The conflict in which Marchbanks defeats Morell was for him a significant stage in the progressive evolution of human culture which it was the business of the imaginative artist to foreknow. But though we may do justice to the seriousness of Shaw's aims, this is not necessarily to accept that he satisfactorily achieved them. If *Arms and the Man* is one of his most deservedly popular plays, the success of *Candida* seems to me much less well deserved. In it Shaw does not himself avoid the qualities he set out to criticise: complacency, sentimentality and spurious idealism.

If in the Unpleasant plays Shaw polemically challenged traditional Victorian ideals and institutions, if in *Arms and the Man* he sent up their absurdity, in *Candida* he adopted a new softly softly approach. In place of slum-landlord or madam, he chose as dramatic antagonist a 'clear, bold, sure, sensible, benevolent, salutarily short-sighted Christian Socialist' (CP, I, 375). 'Salutarily short-sighted' is not necessarily dispraise from a Fabian who believed in the practical doctrine of gradualism, and there is much that is admirable in Morell from Shaw's point of view. He was indeed partly modelled on a personal friend, Rev. Stewart Headlam. If Marchbanks finally rejects the image of the domestic ideal represented by the Morells' marriage, it is given sympathetic treatment as a genuine ideal. Candida is intended to be a woman of real grace and beauty sufficient to inspire Marchbanks to identify her with Titian's principal figure in *The Assumption of the Virgin*. In trying to 'distil the quintessential drama from pre-Raphaelitism', as Shaw somewhat oddly defined his object in *Candida*,[13] 'it must be shewn at its best in conflict with the first broken, nervous, stumbling attempts to formulate its own revolt against itself as it develops into something higher' (CP, I, 373). In other words, we are to respect and admire Morell, Candida and what they stand for, severally and together, and then move on with Marchbanks to a fuller vision of life.

The first act of the play affords us an opportunity to see Morell at his best, surrounded by foils to set him off – the callow curate who attempts to imitate him, the devoted but prickly secretary who adores him, above all his rascally lower-middle-class father-in-law

Burgess. Shaw describes Burgess as 'a man of sixty, made coarse and sordid by the compulsory selfishness of petty commerce, and later on softened into sluggish bumptiousness by overfeeding and commercial success' (CP, I, 525). Morell cuts through his hypocrisy in approved Shavian fashion: 'So long as you come here honestly as a self-respecting, thorough, convinced scoundrel, justifying your scoundrelism and proud of it, you are welcome . . . I like a man to be true to himself, even in wickedness' (CP, I, 530–1). This is the sort of good-humour which is intended to endear Morell to us, as his hatred of economic exploitation and his Christian egalitarianism make us respect him.

Morell's besetting sin, we are to discover, is complacency. To Marchbanks he declares that 'It is easy – terribly easy – to shake a man's faith in himself', but certainly we feel that nothing has happened to shake Morell's faith in himself before. The view of himself as an indulged pet of his wife, the doll of Shaw's male *Doll's House*,[14] is shattering to his completely unquestioned assumption of strength and self-sufficiency. There was in all of this, one suspects, an element of Shavian self-criticism, a revulsion against his own role of lecturer and public figure, his own clarity and confidence of thought. In the opening scene Morell reviews something very like one of Shaw's own crowded diaries of the 1880s and 1890s, with engagements to speak at the Independent Labor Party, the Social-Democratic Federation, and even the Fabian Society. ('Bother the Fabian Society!' says Morell.) When *Arms and the Man* shared the bill with Yeats's fey *Land of Heart's Desire*, it was Shaw's play which was the popular success, Shaw who took the legendary triumphant curtain call. If Yeats was a partial model for Marchbanks, as has sometimes been suggested, then in *Candida* Shaw contrived to show the superiority of the Yeatsian gifts, immature as they were, over what could be taken to be his own. There is finally, however, considerable uncertainty over what we are to feel about Morell. When he has been exposed by Marchbanks as a 'moralist and windbag' it is hard for us to retain any sort of respect for him. The reported rhetoric of his address to the meeting in Act III is so much intoxication, and Shaw marks the point by having all his listeners arrive back drunk. There should be a sense of sympathy with him in the final conflict with Marchbanks for Candida; Shaw tries to give him dignity but achieves only a rather embarrassing pathos. If Shaw intended us to end with a qualified admiration for the 'salutarily short-sighted Christian Socialist', he overreached himself. The play all but annihilates Morell.

This would be allowable if we could believe in the alternative, but Marchbanks' poetics do not represent a credible alternative to Morell's deflated rhetoric. Of course he is supposed to be a very young man and the candy-floss quality of his language is at times intentional, as for instance when he dreams of offering Candida 'a boat: a tiny shallop to sail away in, far from the world, where the marble floors are washed by the rain and dried by the sun; where the south wind dusts the beautiful green and purple carpets' (CP, I, 558). But unfortunately there are other lines which it seems Shaw expected us to approve, and even admire. 'Oh well,' says the typist Proserpine Garnett in pique, 'if you want original conversation, youd better go and talk to yourself.'

> *Marchbanks*: That is what all poets do: they talk to themselves out loud; and the world overhears them. But it's horribly lonely not to hear someone else talk sometimes. (CP, I, 551)

Shaw does not see this as self-pitying attitudinising: it is integral to the idea of the poet which the play dramatises. He is the lone idealist, whose piercing vision isolates him from ordinary people. The climax of the last scene depends on our taking this trite and sentimental idea of the poet seriously. He discovers, or rather Candida discovers for him, that he is stronger than Morell and can do without the support of love. 'He has learnt to live without happiness.' Eugene's exit is pure corn:

> *Candida*: Goodbye. [*She takes his face in her hands; and as he divines her intention and falls on his knees, she kisses his forehead. Then he flies out into the night. She turns to Morell, holding out her arms to him*]. Ah, James!
> > *They embrace. But they do not know the secret in the poet's heart.*
> (CP, I, 594)

The stage directions are the measure of how much Shaw is caught up in the emotional self-indulgence of his characters.

At the root of what is wrong with *Candida* is Candida. There has been considerable controversy over Shaw's attitude towards her, some critics detecting disapproval beneath what others have assumed was whole-hearted enthusiasm.[15] Shaw was certainly impatient with 'Candidamaniacs' who failed to see her tough-mindedness. He intended to show an unscrupulousness, a lack of conventional morality in the model wife and mother who was at the centre of the Victorian ideal of family life. It is not any abstract principle of sexual fidelity which keeps her from giving herself to Marchbanks: 'Ah, James, how little you understand me, to talk of your confidence in my goodness and purity! I would give them both to poor Eugene as willingly as I would give my shawl to a beggar dying of cold, if there were nothing else to restrain me' (CP, I, 565). What motivates Candida is the need to be needed, and she knows finally that Morell needs her more than Marchbanks does. But for all Shaw's impatience with the misunderstanding of Candida's idolaters, he was a Candidamaniac himself. There is adoration in the famous phrase to Ellen Terry, 'Candida, between you and me, is the Virgin Mother and nobody else' (CL, I, 623). Female sexuality was inclined to appear threatening and predatory to Shaw, and there was something specially appealing for him in the secular version of the Virgin Mother, seductive, understanding, protected by taboo from an actual sexual relationship, to be worshipped at arm's length. It is significant that one of the models for Candida was the Lesbian Kate Salt.[16] If there is an undertow of dislike in the play for the possessiveness of Candida, it is to be attributed not to a calculated critique on Shaw's part, but merely to the obverse of his idolisation of the figure.

'A woman like that has divine instinct: she loves our souls, and not our follies and vanities and illusions, nor our collars and coats, nor any other of the rags and tatters we are rolled up in' (CP, I, 578). In its rejection, or evasion of sexuality, *Candida* resembles the traditional Victorianism which it set out to undermine. Shaw's Virgin Mother is not that different from the Angel in the House. When she blacks boots or peels onions, the homeliness is only intended to enhance the radiant charm. The unfortunate Morell is chastised by Shaw for complacency but there is finally a dreadful unacknowledged smugness about Candida. She sits there, the unmoved mover, able to understand both men better than they understand themselves, serene in her patronising self-confidence. 'Let us sit and talk comfortably over it like three friends' (CP, I, 591). The first audiences of *Candida* were not so far wrong when they wept over its sentimental happy ending. The play gave them the reassurance they wanted with the reunion of the happily-married couple brought about not, it is true, by the traditional honourable idealism of the husband, but by a matriarchal control which was quite as comforting.

From the Unpleasant to the Pleasant plays Shaw moved from a radical challenge to playgoers' expectations towards a policy of more subtle sabotage from within conventional dramatic form. There can be little question here of a pragmatic compromise in an effort to get his work produced, though he did try to place several of the Pleasant plays with commercial managements. He remained formidably exacting about the sort of performance he demanded and by 1898 was as far from regular commercial success in London as ever. Shaw moved from Unpleasant to Pleasant plays, from a tactic of confrontation to one of compromise with his audience's expectations, not for practical but for temperamental reasons. Even in the Unpleasant plays, he found it hard to be truly rebarbitive. In the change of tone from *Widowers' Houses* to *Mrs Warren's Profession* we can see his preference for a less offensive dramatic strategy and a pleasanter cast of characters. In *Arms and the Man* he discovered his great gift for stage comedy, and from then on he was determined to put it to use. It was not for him a less serious, a more frivolous form of drama. On the contrary, he declared 'By laughter only can you destroy evil without malice'.[17] This was to be Shaw's aim for the rest of his dramatic career.

In calling his plays Pleasant and Unpleasant, Shaw intended something of the irony of understatememt. After all, rack-renting, philandering and prostitution were not mere unpleasantnesses, nor did he mean *Arms and the Man* and the rest to be taken for pleasantries. He makes clear in the Prefaces the equal purposeful-ness of both volumes, and implicitly mocks the superficiality of such readers as could only categorise them as pleasant and unpleasant. But Shaw ran the risk of having the irony cut against himself, of reaching no deeper than the level of pleasantness or unpleasantness. He declared in his 'Author's Apology' for *Mrs Warren* that the object of the play was to 'produce a very strong and very painful impression of evil' (CP, I, 246). It is hard to know precisely what Shaw means by evil here or in his statement about 'destroying evil without malice'; somewhat later he defined it in deliberately unmetaphysical terms as the errors of the early stages of Creative Evolution.[18] But *Mrs Warren* does not finally produce the very strong and painful impression it might have done because Shaw will not consider the possibility of evil as irremediable. On the other hand, the saccharine sentimentality of *Candida* turned out to be indeed pleasant to a Victorian audience beyond what he intended. In defining the axis of his dramatic work as Pleasant/Unpleasant, Shaw cut himself off from the level of reality bounded by the absolutes of good and evil.

3 Stage Tricks and Suspenses

> My stories are the old stories . . . my stage tricks and suspenses
> and thrills and jests are the ones in vogue when I was a boy, by
> which time my grandfather was tired of them. (Preface to *Three
> Plays for Puritans*, CP, II, 46–7.)

Paradoxical as this claim may have seemed in 1901 when the *Plays
for Puritans* were published, when Shaw was still regarded as the
revolutionary apostle of an unstageable New Drama, it has long
been established as little more than the truth. The techniques by
which Shaw turned older theatrical forms to his own ends have been
demonstrated again and again. Martin Meisel, in particular, has
shown how thoroughly Shaw drew upon the nineteenth-century
theatrical tradition for the very stuff and substance of his plays.[1] The
Plays for Puritans in fact represented Shaw's first deliberate attempt
to write for the commercial theatre in its own terms. The *Unpleasant*
and *Pleasant Plays*, with the exception of *You Never Can Tell* (a
would-be Haymarket farce) and *The Man of Destiny* ('a commercial
traveller's sample'),[2] had all more or less been designed for the new
independent theatre movement. By contrast, *The Devil's Disciple*
was intended as a melodrama for the Adelphi, *Caesar and Cleopatra*
was planned as a vehicle for Johnston Forbes Robertson and Mrs
Patrick Campbell, *Captain Brassbound's Conversion* was Shaw's tribute
to Ellen Terry. All three plays make use of the large stage effects so
popular in the theatre of the time, crowd scenes, tableaux, exotic or
historical settings with eye-catching costumes and backdrops. In
fact, *Caesar and Cleopatra* demanded such a lavish *mise en scène* that the
backing could not initially be found to put it on.[3]

While Shaw still needed defending against the charge that he was
not really a dramatist at all, it seemed necessary to highlight the
theatricality of his work. The research which showed his dependence on popular dramatic forms, along with that which established

37

his practical skills in the theatre, was used as evidence against the old preacher-not-playwright thesis. It should by now be possible to think again about Shaw's theatricality without such controversial ends in mind. The orthodox view, promoted originally by Shaw himself, is that he goes some way towards giving the theatre audience what they expect to see and hear, and then by inverting the expected pattern, or witholding the expected ending, creates his own characteristically Shavian effect. But does it always work like that? Certainly in the case of some of the most popular of Shaw's plays, the audience found it possible to enjoy the traditionally enjoyable, the stage tricks and suspenses, and ignore the iconoclasm. This may have been no more than a conditioned response, but it raises the question of a disjunction in Shaw between the dramatic effect he apparently intended and the theatrical effect he actually achieves. Shaw had a real relish for the histrionic, and at times his theatricality can become pure staginess. In this chapter I want to look at his exploitation of the theatrical in *The Devil's Disciple* and *Caesar and Cleopatra*, to discriminate between those stage effects which are integrated into a significant dramatic pattern and those which are not.

The Devil's Disciple was conceived as melodrama in more than its imitation of stock incidents and formulae – the reading of the will, the rebels versus redcoats, the heroic sacrifice, the last-minute reprieve from the gallows. The play is written in the basic idiom of melodrama, with the shallow characterisation and bold dramatic contrast which are essential principles of the genre. The first entrance of Dick Dudgeon amidst his disapproving relatives sets the mode:

> *Christy (at the window)*: Heres Dick.
>
> *Anderson and Hawkins look round sociably. Essie, with a gleam of interest breaking through her misery, looks up. Christy grins and gapes expectantly at the door. The rest are petrified with the intensity of their sense of Virtue menaced with outrage by the approach of flaunting Vice. The reprobate appears in the doorway, graced beyond his alleged merits by the morning sunlight. He is certainly the best looking of the family; but his expression is reckless and sardonic, his manner defiant and satirical, his dress picturesquely careless. . . .*
>
> *Richard* [*on the threshold, taking off his hat*]: Ladies and gentlemen: your servant, your very humble servant. (CP, II, 70–1)

The play works throughout by means of this sort of arresting and stylised stage composition, and for it Shaw is prepared to forgo subtlety of character. Mrs Dudgeon, for example, who derived from Mrs Clennam in *Little Dorrit*, has little of the depth of the Dickens character. She represents a pure and unrelenting force of repression, hypocritical in her religion, sincere only in her sense of injury and her hatred of joy. In the manuscript draft of the play, she was given lines grimly warning of the likelihood of Dick being hanged like his uncle: 'He may end that way himself, if there is no miracle of grace wrought in him.'[4] The reference to grace would have been appropriate to Mrs Dudgeon's Puritanism, but Shaw was unwilling to grant her even this glimpse of the merciful side of Christianity and cut the line accordingly. Here and throughout the play Shaw gives his characters few shadings, transitions, gradual emotional developments. Everything is immediate and histrionic.

The play is in fact so built around the big theatrical scenes that its success is threatened by such efforts as Shaw did make towards a greater degree of characterisation. General Burgoyne, the one historical figure in the play, whose biography Shaw had read and clearly could not help but admire, looks at one point like running away with the show, by virtue of his sheer strength and specificity of character. This is no more than an incidental imbalance and the play would be much weaker without Burgoyne. Less happy are Shaw's attempts to give a measure of psychological credibility to the Dick–Judith–Anderson triangle which is the play's central design. It is hinted at a number of points in the early scenes that the vehemence of Judith's reaction against Dick is the sign of a repressed attraction. For instance, Anderson addresses a little homily on love and enmity to his wife: 'Come: depend on it, my dear, you are really fonder of Richard than you are of me, if you only knew it' (CP, II, 88). This is intended as a significant joke, preparing us for Judith's romantic attachment to Dick later. But the characters are not conceived with the depth that would have made this sort of implication convincing. Shaw tried a number of times in the manuscript draft of the play's ending to write a scene of *éclaircissement* between Dick and Judith, after Anderson's exit:

> *Judith*: . . . Now I'll tell you something. I never really loved him [Anderson] before: I only pretended to, like most wives. He never could have taught me himself what love is. But you taught me. And now I love *him*. Isn't that funny?
> *Richard*: Quite right. He is a better man than I am.

Judith: But I wish I could have taught you to love too. Is that
   wicked, do you think?
Richard: If it is, then I shall always remain the Devil's Disciple.
Essie: Oh do, dear Dick, please.[5]

But he abandoned this as hopeless and ended the play instead, after
the briefest of exchanges between Dick and Judith, with a
triumphant crowd-scene and Dick chaired from the market-place.

   It was of course one of Shaw's principal aims in *The Devil's
Disciple*, as in the other two *Plays for Puritans*, to challenge the
traditional romantic motivation of the nineteenth-century theatre.
The Devil's Disciple, so superficially true to stereotype, was *not* to be
reformed by the love of a good woman, any more that he was to be
softened by the sight of his old mother. Shaw was indignant at
attempts by both critics and actors to return the play to stock by
reading into Dick's actions a concealed passion for Judith. Now one
critic, Maurice Valency, has argued that it was largely Shaw's fault
if the play was misinterpreted. He had left enough misleading clues
to be picked up, and he had not adequately filled the gap in
motivation left by the removal of a romantic object:

> As Shaw was to find once again in *Pygmalion*, the melodramatic
> forms are not amenable to tinkering. To engage oneself in
> melodrama is, willy-nilly, to abide by its rules. Shaw's plan to
> reform melodrama by means of common sense was doomed from
> the start.[6]

This does not seem to me to represent adequately Shaw's intention
or achievement in the handling of the form.

   The Devil's Disciple is a play about conversion, one of the most
fundamental of Shaw's themes. From *Captain Brassbound*, through
Major Barbara, *Blanco Posnet* and *Pygmalion*, to *Too True to be Good*,
Shaw returned repeatedly to varying forms of inner and outer
transformation or metamorphosis of character. One of the attractions of melodrama for him was its capacity to 'represent conduct as
producing swiftly and certainly on the individual the results which
in actual life it only produces on the race in the course of many
centuries'.[7] Whatever his ideological commitment to the inevit-
ability of gradualness as Fabian and Creative Evolutionist, Shaw
believed firmly in the direct and immediate enactment of change in
the theatre. If we cannot lend even a sympathetic suspension of

disbelief to dramatic conversion, then we can hardly get much from Shaw's work. Of course, the double transformation of *The Devil's Disciple*, the exchange of roles of Anderson and Dick Dudgeon, is implausible in its very symmetry and instantaneousness, but the implausibility heightens the theatrical effect intended. Psychological credibility does not arise as an issue.

Sydney Carton's act of self-sacrifice shadows that of Dick Dudgeon, the Sydney Carton popularised not only by *A Tale of Two Cities* itself but, as Martin Meisel has shown, by several stage adaptations of the novel.[8] Carton does what he does, his 'far far better thing', out of love for Lucy, the wife of his double, Darnay, and out of a conviction of his own worthlessness. Shaw seems to be preparing for a similar image in Dick's reflective speech as he sits having tea with Judith:

> *Richard* [*looking dreamily round*]: I am thinking. It is all so strange to me. I can see the beauty and peace of this home: I think I have never been more at rest in my life than at this moment; and yet I know quite well I could never live here. It's not in my nature, I suppose, to be domesticated. But it's very beautiful: it's almost holy. (CP, II, 94)

This is one of the misleading clues which, Valency argues, justified the misinterpretation of Dick's motives. It does look as though the combination of the beauty of Judith and the sanctity of the home are having the traditional Victorian effect of redeeming the lost soul. But when Dick says that 'it is not in my nature . . . to be domesticated', this is intended to be neither a confession of unworthiness nor a romantic boast, merely a neutral statement of the facts as he then sees them. And when he makes the act of sacrifice it is not *for* Judith, or *for* any other reason but because he discovers then that he is unable to do otherwise. He explains to Judith in Act III:

> You know how much I have lived with worthless men – aye, and worthless women too. Well, they could all rise to some sort of goodness and kindness when they were in love [*the word love comes from him with true Puritan scorn*]. That has taught me to set very little store by the goodness that only comes out red hot. What I did last night, I did in cold blood, caring not half so much for your husband, or [*ruthlessly*] for you [*she droops, stricken*] as I do for myself. I had no motive and no interest: all I can tell you is that

when it came to the point whether I would take my neck out of
the noose and put another man's into it, I could not do it. I dont
know why not: I see myself as a fool for my pains; but I could not
and I cannot. I have been brought up standing by the law of my
own nature; and I may not go against it, gallows or no gallows.
(CP, II, 113)

However much early audiences may have been puzzled by the
unfamiliarity of this against their traditional romantic expectations,
it is surely both strong and convincing in the dramatic context. It
illustrates very strikingly both Dick's Puritanism and Shaw's, the
belief in the inner truth of the individual as a higher source of
inspiration than any attachment to another human being.

The transformation of devil's disciple into martyr in the play is
not a matter of a single turnaround. We see in the final act Dick's
discovery of his true nature continuing as a re-definition of his
attitude of romantic rebellion. There was always an element of pose
in the devil's disciple role as is clear from Shaw's opening
description of him already quoted: 'his expression is reckless and
sardonic, his manner defiant and satirical, his dress picturesquely
careless'. That posing is dropped in the last scenes and we see
instead the underlying character suggested by the rest of Shaw's
description: 'his forehead and mouth betray an extraordinary
steadfastness; and his eyes are the eyes of a fanatic'. Under the
pressure of the trial scene and the imminent sentence of death,
Dick's provocative role-playing becomes a real and fierce defiance,
a mastering anger. The presence of Burgoyne makes this emerge all
the more strongly. Initially there appears to be some degree of
affinity between Dick and Burgoyne. Burgoyne's graceful cynicism,
his contempt for the stupidity and cant of such as Major Swindon,
seem to match him well with Dick, and during the trial they appear
to be enjoying their duel of wit. But Dick in the last scene 'with the
horror of death upon him' will no longer play games:

Hark ye, General Burgoyne. If you think I like being hanged,
youre mistaken. I dont like it; and I dont mean to pretend that I
do. And if you think I'm obliged to you for hanging me in a
gentlemanly way, youre wrong there too. I take the whole
business in devilish bad part; and the only satisfaction I have in it
is that youll feel a good deal meaner than I'll look when it's over.
(CP, II, 135)

He revolts against the mockery of last rites – 'you talk to me of Christianity when you are in the act of hanging your enemies. Was there ever such blasphemous nonsense!' There are no tender farewells with Judith, but a horrified rejection: 'Take her away. Do you think I want a woman near me now?' Shaw uses the gallows-scene not, *à la* Sydney Carton, for a frozen tableau of heroic self-sacrifice, but for a forceful and vivid evocation of the extreme mood of a man in this extremity. Of course we know that the reprieve is coming, that Anderson will reappear in the nick of time but, as in all melodrama, we feel the suspense as if that were not certain, and we believe in Dick as someone really facing death.

The reprieve supplies not only the happy ending necessary to the melodrama but the Shavian explication of its meaning:

> Anderson [*between Judith and Richard*]: Sir: it is in the hour of trial that a man finds his true profession. This foolish young man [*placing his hand on Richard's shoulder*] boasted himself the Devil's Disciple; but when the hour of trial came to him, he found that it was his destiny to suffer and be faithful to the death. I thought myself a decent minister of the gospel of peace; but when the hour of trial came to me, I found that it was my destiny to be a man of action, and that my place was amid the thunder of the captains and the shouting. So I am starting life at fifty as Captain Anthony Anderson of the Springtown militia; and the Devil's Disciple here will start presently as the Reverend Richard Dudgeon, and wag his pow in my old pulpit, and give good advice to this silly sentimental little wife of mine. (CP, II, 139)

We cannot imagine Dick Dudgeon literally taking Anderson's place as minister, and the hint that Anderson is handing over his wife as well as his job hardly seems acceptable. But it is an appropriately bold and exaggerated way of underscoring the change of roles represented emblematically by the time-honoured theatrical device of the change of coats. Once again the relative crudeness of the stage effect works to express a fundamental Shavian theme. One stage version of *A Tale of Two Cities* was called *The Only Way*; Shaw's *Devil's Disciple* might have been called *The Two Ways*. The way of action and the way of suffering, embodied in Anderson and Dick Dudgeon, remained for Shaw the alternative roads to salvation. Shaw's impatience with 'Crosstianity', his consistent emphasis on the need of goodness for what Cashel Byron calls 'executive power', show his temperamental bias in favour of the way of action. But it seems to me a misreading of *The Devil's Disciple* to see in it 'the dramatist's imaginative progress from the strong attraction of a romantic rebel pose (Dick Dudgeon) to an antithetical attitude of cheerful, energetic and aggressive practicality (Anthony Anderson)'.[9] Dick condemns himself as a fool for what he has done, but Shaw does not invite us to share in that condemnation. It is truly in the nature of some 'to suffer and be faithful to the death', and Shaw respects that nature, even against his own preference for practical action. Against Ferrovius in *Androcles and the Lion*, the militant Christian who finds Christian pacificism impossible, there is Androcles himself. Shaw's admiration for Saint Joan is for her martyrdom as much as her soldiership.

The Devil's Disciple is not a parody of melodrama but it is at times close to pastiche – the self-conscious use of a style which is not the author's own. It is one of the few plays of Shaw which is not thoroughly Shavianised in style and action. It was partly for this reason that he was so impatient with those who preferred it to what were, for him, more significant and characteristic works. He protested vigorously to Mrs Richard Mansfield, whose husband had made such a success with *The Devil's Disciple* in America:

> you may NOT say that you like the Devil's Disciple better than 'C & C'. The D's D is a melodrama, made up of all the stale Adelphi tricks. . . . Anybody could make a play that way. But 'C & C' is the first & only adequate dramatization of the greatest man that ever lived. (CL, II, 89–90)

The annoyance is understandable; *The Devil's Disciple* was a limited work which did not tax Shaw's creative powers, whereas *Caesar and Cleopatra* was his first major play of ideas. And yet within its limits *The Devil's Disciple* works, because there is a coincidence between what Shaw really wanted to say dramatically and the theatrical means he found to say it, while *Caesar and Cleopatra* exposes difficulties in the use of the theatrical which the slighter play does not.

'The first and only *adequate* dramatization of the greatest man that ever lived': a principal motivation behind the play was Shaw's strong feeling of the *inadequacy* of Shakespeare's dramatisation of Julius Caesar. Shakespeare, Shaw complained, wrote 'Caesar down for the merely technical purpose of writing Brutus up' (CP, II, 39). In his play he was determined to give Caesar the centre stage which Shakespeare had denied him, to explore the 'human strength of the Caesarian type' which he argued Shakespeare failed to understand. At the same time his *Caesar and Cleopatra* was planned as a protest against *Antony and Cleopatra:*

> Shakespear's Antony and Cleopatra must needs be as intolerable to the true Puritan as it is vaguely distressing to the ordinary healthy citizen, because, after giving a faithful picture of the soldier broken down by debauchery, and the typical wanton in whose arms such men perish, Shakespear finally strains all his huge command of rhetoric and stage pathos to give a theatrical sublimity to the wretched end of the business, and to persuade foolish spectators that the world was well lost by the twain. (CP, II, 37)

It hardly needs to be pointed out that it was Dryden not Shakespeare who subtitled his play *The World Well Lost*, or that the ending of *Antony and Cleopatra* is much more ambiguous than Shaw makes it sound. For him it remained a meretricious play, glamourising irresponsibility, and all the more irritating for the immense theatrical power with which the glamourising is done. The relationship between Caesar and Cleopatra which he set out to show was to be specifically not a sexual one. (All the historical evidence to the contrary – Caesar's notorious reputation as a womaniser, Cleopatra's visit to Rome, Caesarion, her supposed son by Caesar – Shaw simply ignores.)[10] It is the measure of the Shavian Caesar's superiority that he never comes near losing his head for Cleopatra, and the measure of her limitation that she should prefer Antony.

Shaw plays upon his audience's familiarity with Shakespeare throughout *Caesar and Cleopatra*. The insistent echoes and parallels amount to large-scale theatrical quotation. When at the end of Act I Caesar arranges Cleopatra's enrobing we are conscious that this is the beginning of the story which ends with 'Give me my robe, put on my crown; I have Immortal longings in me'. When in Act III Cleopatra, concealed in the carpet, is hauled up by pulleys to Caesar, Shakespeare's Monument scene with Cleopatra and her attendants hauling up the wounded Antony is in our minds. As Shakespeare's Cleopatra playfully helps to arm Antony, so Shaw's

Cleopatra helps to arm Caesar. Shakespeare's plays generated
Shaw's in all sorts of major and minor ways. Caesar's spirited
challenge of Rufio to a swimming-race as he prepares to leap into
Alexandria harbour, stands against the satiric anecdote of the
swimming-contest in the Tiber told by Cassius to belittle Caesar
(*Julius Caesar*, I, ii). The character of Rufio himself, the type of the
honest, cynical, direct Roman soldier, is very obviously derived
from Shakespeare's Enobarbus.

Yet in many of these instances Shaw's theatrical effects simply live
off their Shakespearean counterparts; they do not correct, alter or
invert the images from which they are derived. It is true that at
times we are conscious of an exemplary contrast between Shaw's
Caesar and Shakespeare's Antony. There is a marked reproof of
Antony's behaviour at Actium when Caesar prepares to leave
Cleopatra to go into battle: 'of my soldiers who have trusted me
there is not one whose hand I shall not hold more sacred than your
head' (CP, II, 246). But more often the Shakespearean echoes serve
only as artificial amplification of Shaw's scenes, giving them an
inherited power which they have not earned dramatically. *Caesar
and Cleopatra* is in many cases directly dependent on that 'theatrical
sublimity' which, Shaw argued, Shakespeare so misused in *Antony
and Cleopatra*. What is more, sometimes Shaw even follows
Shakespeare in the bathetic treatment of Caesar of which he
ostensibly disapproved. An obvious feature of Shakespeare's portrait of Julius Caesar is the technique by which every boastful
assertion of superiority is punctured by a reminder of physical
frailty. But Shaw is not above using Caesar's baldness as
Shakespeare used his deafness; and there is nothing so devastatingly
anticlimactic in *Julius Caesar* as the unseen and unidentified
Cleopatra's interruption of Caesar's grandly pretentious address to
the Sphinx:

> My way hither was the way of destiny; for I am he of whose
> genius you are the symbol: part brute, part woman, and part
> god – nothing of man in me at all. Have I read your riddle,
> Sphinx?
> *The Girl* [*who has wakened, and peeped cautiously from her nest to see who
> is speaking*]: Old gentleman. (CP, II, 182)

Right through the play, Shaw exploits the gap in age between
Caesar and Cleopatra not only to remove the possibility of a sexual
relationship between them but to mortify Caesar.

Shaw was contemptuous of the popular image of history as conditioned by Shakespeare's plays:

> The only way to write a play which shall convey to the general public an impression of antiquity is to make the characters speak blank verse and abstain from reference to steam, telegraphy, or any of the material conditions of their existence. (CP, II, 294)

He denied that there was anything anachronistic about his *Caesar and Cleopatra*, though the characters spoke modern prose and talked about the same issues as late nineteenth-century Victorians. The ground of his defence against the charge of anachronism was that human beings would not have changed essentially between the time of Caesar and the time of Shaw. The ancient Egyptian guardsman in the opening stage direction of the Alternative to the Prologue 'has just finished telling a naughty story (still current in English barracks)' (CP, II, 168). Although Shaw believed in change and progress, he argued in the Notes to *Caesar and Cleopatra* that two millennia as too short a section of the history of the human race to make any noticeable difference. He mocks the idea of the scholarly historian painfully reconstructing a past alien to his own. A dead-pan programme note for the copyright performance in 1899 gave an enormous list of historical authorities, ancient and modern, and ended with the punch-line, 'Many of these authorities have consulted their imaginations, more or less. The author has done the same' (CP, II, 306).

However, the dramatic imagination of a historical action is not, as Shaw implies, a simple matter of treating Caesar and Cleopatra as our contemporaries, and the problem of finding a credible style for his Romans and Egyptians is not one he solved altogether successfully. The weakness of the self-consciously modern portrayal of historical figures is that time moves on and the updated comes to look merely dated. Nothing seems more arch and unconvincing by now than Shaw's references to Art for Art's sake or the New Woman in *Caesar and Cleopatra*. Brittanus, the ancient Briton as precursor of the Victorian Briton, with all his hypocritical and imperialistic moralism, is by now supremely unfunny. But there is, besides, a fundamental uncertainty as to style deriving from the awareness of the play's historical setting. The main characters, and Caesar in particular, are given standard Shavian dialogue, much of it very accomplished Shavian dialogue. They are indeed contemporaries, cousins of John Tanner and Ann Whitefield, Undershaft and Major Barbara. But the supporting characters have no such security of speech. Much of the dialogue of the Egyptians is stage Oriental at its stagiest – all 'thous' and 'thees' and effusive apostrophe. Ftatateeta, an important enough character for it to matter, has particularly excruciating lines. And on the other side, for sheer melodramatic banality Rufio's exclamation when he learns that the Romans are surrounded would take beating: 'Curses! It is true. We are caught like rats in a trap' (CP, II, 247). The reason for such lapses is that Shaw is bothered by the foreignness and historical remoteness of his setting, and tends to fall back on the sort of ham language which normally he would have despised.

Shaw worked very hard to *dramatise* the history of Caesar and Cleopatra but it did not come easily or naturally to him. 'I can make no headway with C & C', he wrote to Charles Charrington in October 1898. 'Can't get any drama out of the story – nothing but comedy & character' (CL, II, 65). The third act of the play written at around this time can be seen as Shaw's self-conscious attempt to overcome this problem. It centres around the Cleopatra carpet escapade, the one episode that most people would have been likely to remember from the story of Caesar and Cleopatra, and therefore necessarily to be included in any play on the subject. The isolation of Caesar and his men on the Pharos, the suspense of trying to reach them, the bravura of Apollodorus and the concluding dives into the harbour, are all intended to contribute to an effect of theatrical excitement. Yet when Shaw allowed this act to be cut altogether, indeed insisted that it rather than any other part of the play be sacrificed to reduce the whole to playable length, he tacitly acknowledged that it was not integral to the dramatic development.[11] It does not advance the understanding of the characters of Caesar and Cleopatra and it is thus not much more than a theatrical diversion, in some danger, as Shaw himself felt, of distracting the audience from the more central issues of the fourth act.

The fourth act, from Shaw's point of view, was crucial to the success of the play. It affords the fullest opportunity for Caesar to put forward his Shavian world-view in striking contrast to those around him; but it was also planned as a climax to the dramatic action. The scene of the banquet on the roof-garden which makes up the bulk of the act was conceived as a theatrical spectacular. Shaw took great care with the set-design, making possible a breathtaking moment when the curtained-off upstage area is revealed:

The curtains are drawn, revealing the roof garden with a banqueting table set across in the middle for four persons, one at each end, and two side by side. The side next Caesar and Rufio is blocked with golden wine vessels and basins. A gorgeous majordomo is superintending the laying of the table by a staff of slaves. The colonnade goes round the garden at both sides to the further end, where a gap in it, like a great gateway, leaves the view open to the sky beyond the western edge of the roof, except in the middle, where a life size image of Ra, seated on a huge plinth, towers up, with hawk head and crown of asp and disk. His altar, which stands at his feet, is a single white stone. (CP, II, 262)

Against this flamboyant background of theatrical picturesque, the contrast between the luxurious and exotic Egyptians and Caesar's Roman austerity is developed.

The offstage murder of Pothinus sinisterly alters the atmosphere from the festive mood of the banquet to the grim sequel. Shaw is heading towards the strong conclusion of the act when Cleopatra, left alone, calls to her nurse/murderess:

Ftatateeta. Ftatateeta. It is dark; and I am alone. Come to me. [*Silence*] Ftatateeta. [*Louder*] Ftatateeta. [*Silence. In a panic she snatches the cord and pulls the curtains apart*].

Ftatateeta is lying dead on the alter of Ra, with her throat cut. Her blood deluges the white stone. (CP, II, 283)

Shaw intended more by this than mere melodramatics. There is an important discussion in the final act, in which Caesar discriminates ethically between the bloodlust that motivated the murder of Pothinus by Cleopatra and Ftatateeta, and Rufio's elimination of the latter 'without malice'. The tone is finally lightened by a return to the old joke about Ftatateeta's unpronounceable name. But Act IV is still grand guignol and it is not a congenial mode for Shaw. There is something repulsive because unreal in the directions which Shaw uses to describe Cleopatra and Ftatateeta after the murder:

Caesar glancing at Cleopatra, catches her pouring out her wine before the god, with gleaming eyes, and mute assurances of gratitude and worship . . .

Ftatateeta comes back by the far end of the roof, with dragging steps, a drowsy satiety in her eyes and in the corners of the bloodhound lips. For a moment Caesar suspects that she is drunk with wine. Not so Rufio: he knows well the red vintage that has inebriated her. (CP, II, 272–3)

This is not a genuinely macabre imagination, it is no more than cheap horror-mongering. Like so much in *Caesar and Cleopatra* it is stagey rather than truly dramatic because it is conceived as stage effect rather than as part of any more deeply felt dramatic experience.

What really interested Shaw in writing *Caesar and Cleopatra* was the character of Caesar himself, 'the greatest man that ever lived'. In fact the play amounts to a series of more or less successful attempts to make things happen to demonstrate the nature of his central character. Shaw complained that Shakespeare sacrificed Caesar to magnify Brutus, but he sacrificed Cleopatra to Caesar. It was the glorification of Cleopatra in the last act of *Antony and Cleopatra* which most offended Shaw, and in his play he set out to cut her down to size. He jeered at the audience drawn by her name in the Prologue: 'Do ye crave for a story of an unchaste woman? Hath the name of Cleopatra tempted ye hither? Ye foolish ones; Cleopatra is as yet but a child that is whipped by her nurse' (CP, II, 166). The picture of Cleopatra in the first act is indeed of a half-grown child, wilful, superstitious, sadistic. Shaw has projected backwards Shakespeare's passionate Cleopatra and shown some of her most obvious characteristics in the antics of a sixteen-year-old girl.

Shaw was sure that the relationship between his Caesar and his Cleopatra would not be a sexual one, but he seems to have been unsure just what alternative sort of relationship it would be. Caesar, though not infatuated with the Egyptian queen like Shakespeare's Antony, has a weakness for her and is hurt by the fact that she regards him in a wholly paternal light. Yet ultimately his feelings for her are so unimportant that he nearly forgets to say goodbye to her before leaving Egypt. Cleopatra hero-worships Caesar, and in the first scene of Act IV we are shown the effect of that hero-worship as a moral education. She has, she tells Pothinus, been changed by daily contact with Caesar:

When I was foolish, I did what I liked, except when Ftatateeta beat me; and even then I cheated her, and did it by stealth. Now that Caesar has made me wise, it is no use my liking or disliking: I do what must be done, and have not time to attend to myself. That is not happiness; but it is greatness. (CP, II, 256)

This is the Shavian doctrine of the will of which Caesar is one of the main exemplars. But in the murder of Pothinus which follows, Cleopatra shows that she has not been reclaimed by Caesar's influence, and in her final longing for Antony in place of Caesar, Shaw implies that she is irreclaimable.

If conversion is one major Shavian theme, education is another nearly allied. The relationship between Caesar and Cleopatra is in some ways a pre-run of the relationship of Higgins and Eliza. But in the later play Shaw caught the complexity and ambiguity of the master/pupil, Pygmalion/Galathea attraction. In *Pygmalion* he showed Eliza transformed by Higgins, Higgins caught by his own creature, and the convincing human stalemate that resulted. In *Caesar and Cleopatra* Shaw both wanted to show Caesar's personality as strong enough to change a Cleopatra, but also to reveal Cleopatra as incapable of change. In his anxiety to avoid a romantic treatment of the pair, he comes close to denying that there is a significant relationship between them at all, and thus eliminating the subject of the play.

Shaw was not happy with *Caesar and Cleopatra*; at least there is a letter to William Archer (CL, II, 93–5) in which he admits that Archer's sense of dissatisfaction with the play has some justification. But he claims that it was the nature of the historical material which made the play formally unsatisfactory, the need of the chronicle to get in sufficient information to account for a complicated historical situation. This does not seem to me convincing. Shaw took all the liberties he wanted with the historical material, and included a whole act which does not advance the chronicle in the least for pure theatrical effect. What is actually wrong with *Caesar and Cleopatra* is that it does not have a real dramatic dynamic animating the action throughout. Shaw wrote it partly in an attempt to revive the heroic drama, specifically to provide a great heroic role in the modern idiom (see CP, II, 306–10). But he could not find a proper vehicle for the role of Caesar as he conceived it. Although superficially in revolt against Shakespeare, he is forced to borrow theatrical éclat from Shakespeare. His efforts to produce colourful, spectacular, histrionic effects to support the heroic mode tended to result in *papier mâché*. The theatrical demands of *Caesar and Cleopatra* as Shaw designed it worked finally to sabotage its coherence and dramatic integrity.

Shaw was a great man of the theatre; that should now be established, accepted, proven beyond dispute. But Shaw's theatricality, though it is fundamental to his success as a playwright and has helped to keep his plays on the stage for so long, can also be a source of weakness in his work, and not only in the self-consciously theatrical *Caesar and Cleopatra*. A play such as *The Doctor's Dilemma* also depends upon false theatrical effects which it is ostensibly intended to combat. As a satire it implies a traditional comic scepticism about the pretensions of science and medicine, yet we are required to believe in Ridgeon's wonder-drug as a *donnée* of the plot. The suspense of the doctor's dilemma, the histrionics of Dubedat's death Shaw attempts to treat both ironically and unironically, and the result is an impression of artistic disingenuousness. Right through Shaw's work there are scenes of pure hamming which are included simply to thrill and delight the audience as, one suspects, at some level they thrilled and delighted Shaw. But they are out of key with the main mode of Shavian dramatic representation and as such they seem artificial and unreal concessions to popular taste – stage tricks and suspenses knowingly and artfully worked by a playwright who knows better.

4 Comedy and Dialectic

Having completed *Captain Brassbound's Conversion*, the last of the *Plays for Puritans*, Shaw announced his (temporary) retirement from the theatre in a letter to Ellen Terry:

> And now no more plays – at least no more practicable ones. None at all, indeed, for some time to come: it is time to do something more in Shaw-philosophy, in politics & sociology. Your author, dear Ellen, must be more than a common dramatist. (CL, II, 96)

However, writing *Man and Superman* was not so much a new departure for him, as the fulfilment of an ambition conceived before he had even begun his career as a 'common dramatist'. Already in 1889, explaining his abandonment of the novel, he described the new form he wanted to develop instead:

> Sometimes in spare moments I write dialogues; and these are all working up to a certain end (a sermon, of course) my imagination playing the usual tricks meanwhile of creating visionary persons &c. When I have a few hundred of these dialogues worked up and interlocked, then a drama will be the result – a moral, instructive, suggestive comedy of modern society, guaranteed correct in philosophic and economic detail, and unactably independent of theatrical considerations. (CL, I, 222)

This reads like a blueprint for *Man and Superman*. Nothing is more remarkable about Shaw than the clarity with which he could conceive such a project long before it was realised; one can almost believe that *Man and Superman* was not written until 1901–2 only because he has not enough 'spare moments' to write it before then.

When his 'comedy and philosophy' was published in 1903 it confirmed most critics in their opinion that Shaw was no dramatist. Max Beerbohm in the *Saturday Review* was representative: 'This peculiar article is, of course, not a play at all. It is "as good as a play" – infinitely better, to my peculiar taste, than any play I have ever read or seen enacted. But a play it is not.'[1] Yet, although Shaw had planned something 'unactably independent of theatrical considerations', directed not towards any actual audience but a hypothetical 'pit of philosophers', he was incapable of producing anything in dramatic form which was untheatrical. As he himself said, 'no man writes a play without any reference to the possibility of performance' (CP, II, 308), and the introduction of the motor-car must have been designed with a view to the *coup de théâtre* to be created on stage by its spectacular exit at the end of Act II. The performance of *Man and Superman* and *Don Juan in Hell* separately in 1905 and 1907, and productions of the entire work since, have proved that it is by no means unactable.[2] Indeed Shaw felt that the play's very success on stage made it a partial failure in terms of what he had conceived. *Man and Superman*, he claimed in the Preface to *Back to Methuselah*, was 'a dramatic parable of Creative Evolution' which had got lost in the brilliance of the comedy. 'The effect was so vertiginous, apparently, that nobody noticed the new religion in the centre of the intellectual whirlpool' (CP, V, 338). Accordingly in *Back to Methuselah* he omitted the distractions and wrote a 'cycle of plays that keep to the point all through' (CP, V, 339).

Only the most hard-bitten and committed of Shavians would be prepared to accept that the more purely doctrinaire *Back to Methuselah* represents an improvement on the hybrid *Man and Superman*. The 'metabiological pentateuch' does indeed 'keep to the point all through' to a devastating degree. But the mixed form of 'comedy and philosophy' in the earlier play remains problematic. To what extent is it one at the expense of the other – a Platonic dialogue masquerading as a play, as Beerbohm suggested, or an over-successful comedy with its success obscuring its philosophical purpose, as Shaw himself claimed? I would argue that it is neither, that the comedy and the philosophy interlock and interpenetrate all but perfectly. Indeed it seems to me that its very coherence, the unity of its conception and design, constitute its major limitation. Although Shaw never wrote a play quite like *Man and Superman* again, it is central to his work, and the analysis of its unique form is of crucial importance in assessing the nature of his comedy of ideas.

The homogeneousness of *Man and Superman* is striking considering the heterogeneousness of its origins. No play better illustrates Shaw's image of himself as a crow that has followed many ploughs, hopping 'hungry and curious, across the fields of philosophy, politics, and art' (CP, II, 47). In the Epistle Dedicatory to *Man and Superman* he lists a whole pantheon of artists and thinkers 'whose peculiar sense of the world I recognise as more or less akin to my own' with the implication that they all influenced the play. Among major ideological sources are Schopenhauer, Nietzsche and Samuel Butler; among formal models may be counted Mozart, Plato and Blake, but critics have identified many other likely influences.[3] The Shavian synthesis produced from this unlikely and diverse range of materials represents a triumph of building and blending skills.

I suggested in the first chapter that Shaw's object from early on in his career was to harness the energies of comedy. In *Man and Superman* he set out to identify those energies, to define them explicitly within the play. We have not a comedy plus a philosophy, but rather a comedy philosophised. It is generally agreed that one of Shaw's main sources for the play was the chapter entitled 'The Metaphysics of the Love of the Sexes' in Schopenhauer's *The World as Will and Idea*.[4] From this he derived the notion that individual sexual attraction was in fact a manifestation of an instinctive impulse of the race. But Shaw followed Schopenhauer not only in the specific concept of love, but in the object of supplying a metaphysics for the sexual relationship. Schopenhauer introduces his chapter by remarking that love, the overwhelming concern of poets and dramatists through the ages, has never been seriously considered by philosophers. He claims to be establishing for the first time a metaphysics of sexuality. Shaw similarly wished to reveal the ideological underpinning which might be detected in the traditional treatment of love and marriage in comedy.

It is this purpose of supplying it with an ideology which is the outstandingly original feature of *Man and Superman* as love-comedy. For all the iconoclasm of a Don Juan who is the pursued rather than the pursuer, the comic action of *Man and Superman* is not in itself all that unorthodox. In most love-comedies, even the most romantic, there is an anti-romantic strain implied in the form itself. Love is seen as a blind force controlling the characters, and the comedian exploits the ironic disparity between the apparent individuality of feeling expressed by the lovers and the sense that such feelings are universal and impersonal. The bed-trick, Shakespeare's identical twins, are archetypal devices used to suggest the interchangeability of love-objects. Love, sex and marriage in comedy are parts of a more or less cynically viewed social ritual in which individual impulse works always towards ends which are none of its own. What Shaw identifies as the Life Force in *Man and Superman* is no more than the shaping natural providence implicit in the probable and improbable multiple marriages at the end of so many traditional comedies.

If the idea of a metaphysics for sexual attraction may be derived from Schopenhauer, however, the full theory developed in *Man and Superman* is not. For Schopenhauer, at least in the 'Metaphysics of the Love of the Sexes', the highest type of love was expressed in the most fully mutual passion, though that passion when consummated was likely to end in unhappy marriage.[5] In Schopenhauer it is the will of the man which meets the intellect of the woman. With Shaw it is the woman who exercises the will, her own and that of the Life Force, and man the intellectual who tries to escape from it. There were, no doubt, personal reasons for Shaw's insistence on this image of the battle of the sexes with the reluctant male and the female aggressor. In *The Philanderer* already, writing directly out of his own experience, he had developed the figure of the hunted philosopher/ hero. But even acknowledging this idiosyncratic bias, John Tanner and Ann Whitefield are not fundamentally out of line with the lovers of traditional comedy. Tanner is the type of the comic figure who defies the power of love and must be humbled into marriage. Ann, superficially docile and conventional, in fact wily and disingenuous in pursuit of her love, corresponds to a certain type of comic heroine. Once again it is not the battle of the sexes in *Man and Superman* which differentiates it from other comedies but Shaw/Tanner's continuous theoretical commentary upon it.

Nietzsche takes over where Schopenhauer leaves off in the ideological structure of *Man and Superman*. If the English language owes the word 'superman' to Shaw, Shaw owed the concept to Nietzsche. According to Schopenhauer the human species itself was infinite; anything beyond it was unthinkable. Indeed the perpetuation of the species which was the implacable object of the will to live manifested in sexual attraction was, for him, a source of despair. Shaw's Life Force may have been based on Schopenhauer's World Will,[6] but its positive evolutionary character was shaped by Samuel Butler, and its ultimate goal was the Nietzschean superman. The revelation of the doctrine of the superman is the main aim of the dream interlude, *Don Juan in Hell*. It is the final philosophic plane which it is the function of the comedy to reach. There is no necessary connection between the idea of the Life Force as the motive power of sexual attraction, the duel of the sexes, and the concept of the superman. Yet Shaw welds them into a single ideological pattern. Both man and woman, John Tanner and Ann Whitefield, must serve the Life Force. His reluctance, her aggression are essential attributes of their several roles: he as intellectual, as independent mind, strives to escape from the tyranny of physical love and the personal subjection of marriage; she as the principle of vitality must use him to fulfil her creative purpose. Both together are instruments in the evolution of the race. The individuality and intellectual aspiration which makes Tanner resist marriage is precisely what attracts Ann to him as the 'father for the superman'.

Shaw not only creates an ideological unity out of the most disparate strands of thought but he uses all his dramatist's gifts to integrate his philosophy with his comedy. The social comedy of Acts I, II, and IV works as the embodiment and expression of many of the play's ideas, while the discursive debate in Hell which makes up most of Act III is controlled with a comedian's skills of pace and timing. In the main plot Shaw's strategy with his hero/spokesman was to make him a comic figure who is always right, and yet always contrives to get everything wrong. One of the funniest scenes in the play is Tanner's impassioned defence of Violet's supposedly unmarried pregnancy in Act I. Shaw uses the incident – brought in with cheerful lack of preparation or relevance – to hit off all the absurdities of the conventional attitude towards illicit sexuality.

> *Octavius*: But who is the man? He can make reparation by marrying her; and he shall, or he shall answer for it to me.
> *Ramsden*: He shall, Octavius. There you speak like a man.
> *Tanner*: Then you dont think him a scoundrel, after all?
> *Octavius*: Not a scoundrel! He is a heartless scoundrel.
> *Ramsden*: A damned scoundrel. I beg your pardon, Annie; but I can say no less.
> *Tanner:* So we are to marry your sister to a damned scoundrel by way of reforming her character! On my soul, I think you are all mad. (CP, II, 562)

Tanner is given an eloquent speech in defence of unmarried motherhood. But all of this leads up to the comic revelation of Violet's marriage and her acerbic rejection of his championship:

Violet [*flushing with indignation*]: Oh! You think me a wicked
woman, like the rest. You think I have not only been vile, but
that I share your abominable opinions. Miss Ramsden: I have
borne your hard words because I knew you would be sorry for
them when you found out the truth. But I wont bear such a
horrible insult as to be complimented by Jack on being one of
the wretches of whom he approves. I have kept my marriage
secret for my husband's sake. But now I claim my right as a
married woman not to be insulted. (CP, II, 582)

Jack is left 'in ruins', the victim of the traditional comic nemesis
visited upon those who show excess enthusiasm or bravado.

And yet Jack, here and throughout the play, is right – at least he
expresses an exaggerated and flamboyant version of his author's
views. His identification of Ann as the husband-huntress, the agent
of the Life Force, is of course correct; it is only his idea that her
quarry is Octavius rather than himself which is mistaken. His great
tirade against mothers in Act II is a vehement denunciation of the
fashionable marriage-market:

Oh, I protest against this vile abjection of youth to age! Look at
fashionable society as you know it. What does it pretend to be? An
exquisite dance of nymphs. What is it? A horrible procession of
wretched girls, each in the claws of a cynical, cunning, avaricious,
disillusioned, ignorantly experienced, foul-minded old woman
whom she calls mother, and whose duty it is to corrupt her mind
and sell her to the highest bidder. (CP, II, 598–9)

But he is so carried away with his indignation that he issues what he
intends to be a merely rhetorical invitation to Ann to defy mother
and convention by driving across Europe with him, and finds himself
promptly and devastatingly accepted. Many critics have argued
that the comic treatment of Tanner makes our reaction to his ideas
an ironical one. I feel rather that Shaw's object is to make us laugh at
the speechifying, not necessarily at what the speeches say. Tanner
the thinker who yet cannot see where his thought may be taking him
in the real world is not only a stock comic type – the astronomer who
falls into the pit – but an illustration of Shaw's doctrine of the artist-
man who must submit to the practical will of the woman.

The dream debate in Hell, the most explicitly philosophical part
of the play, is in fact a *jeu d'esprit* put to extraordinary Shavian ends.

Its tone is that of an eschatological joke. It combines schoolboyish irreverence with the reassuring comic bathos of discovering that life after death is quite a comfortable affair. We laugh as Doña Ana is disabused of her conventional notions of Heaven and Hell, angels and harps, devils and torments. There are mischievous cracks at the great literary images of the underworld and the afterlife. The Devil describes the misconceptions of his kingdom derived from

> two of the greatest fools that ever lived, an Italian and an Englishman. The Italian described it as a place of mud, frost, filth, fire, and venomous serpents: all torture. This ass, when he was not lying about me, was maundering about some woman whom he saw once in the street. The Englishman described me as being expelled from Heaven by cannons and gunpowder; and to this day every Briton believes that the whole of his silly story is in the Bible. (CP, II, 655)

He cites the Book of Job as evidence of the fact that, so far from being irrevocably banished from Heaven, he can visit it as often as he wants.

Shaw called himself 'a pupil of Mozart in comedy much more than of any of the English literary dramatists'.[7] But *Don Giovanni* is used in *Man and Superman* almost wholly for purposes of parody, diversion, comic relief. For all Shaw's ingenious arguments in the Epistle Dedicatory, his Don Juan has little significant relation to Mozart's or anyone else's. Instead we get a series of running gags based on anticlimactic inversion of the characters and attitudes of the opera. After the dramatic music of the Commendatore, appears the very urbane statue who excuses himself from singing the part Mozart wrote for him, explaining that he is unfortunately a counter-tenor rather than a bass. The Commendatore and Don Juan, even the unseen Don Ottavio, much to Doña Ana's indignation, are very good friends in the afterlife. Don Juan's murder of the Commendatore is reduced to farce by the latter's insistence that he was the better swordsman and would have killed Don Juan but for an accident. These recurrent jokes are used to punctuate and puncture the long speeches of Juan and the Devil which constitute the main substance of the dream debate. They serve as comic counterpoint to the Shavian dialectic.

Yet if Shaw disposes comically of the traditional supernatural view of the hereafter, it is to clear the ground for his own conception of salvation and damnation. He dispels the notion of Heaven and Hell as places of reward and retribution; goodness or evil meeting the recompense of happiness or pain do not come into it for Shaw. The Shavian distinction between salvation and damnation is a pure value-judgement on different human states of mind in the here and now. It is the difference between living life as though it had a purpose and living it as though it had none beyond the enjoyment of life itself. To live for pleasure only, however sophisticated or apparently humane that pleasure may be, is to be damned, and an eternity of such pleasure-seeking is literally Shaw's idea of Hell. Heaven by contrast is not so much a place of pure and beatific contemplation as a place of directed thought. 'To be in hell is to drift: to be in heaven is to steer.' The debate between Juan and the Devil is between the affirmation and the denial of life, or rather the purposefulness of life. The Devil believes, in the great tradition of philosophical pessimism, that there is 'nothing new under the sun'. In 'reform, progress, fulfilment of upward tendency' he sees 'nothing but an infinite comedy of illusion' (CP, II, 683). It is the ideological position with which Shaw quarelled all his life, most notably as he saw it represented in Shakespeare, and he uses Juan as his spokesman to set against it a teleology for man and the universe. For all the force of the Devil's great speech on man's love of death, Juan maintains with Shaw's full backing that there is purpose and meaning in the world, and that a Life Force works in and through man towards consummation in the superman.

Man and Superman is a single-minded play and, in spite of all its philosophical borrowings, there is no doubting that the single mind is Shaw's. The whole enormous work with all its appendages – Epistle Dedicatory and Revolutionist's Handbook – is essentially univocal, even monolithic. This is perhaps why it does not read like the modernist piece which it superficially resembles in form. In its ironic treatment of a great literary myth, in its philosophical underpinning, in its use of multiple modes, *Man and Superman* would seem to conform to the characteristic methods of modernism. One critic at least has tried to argue that it should be seen in the broad context of the symbolist movement of the late nineteenth and early twentieth centuries.[8] But analogies with a work such as, say, Strindberg's *Dream Play* seem inappropriate.[9] Shaw's play follows through with the cohesiveness and cogency of argument; it has none of Strindberg's apparent randomness of progression, his exploitation of irrational dream logic. There is nothing elliptical, nothing merely suggestive, nothing opaque in *Man and Superman*.

This is the more striking if one contrasts Shaw's methods and effects with those of writers whom he was more or less consciously following in different parts of the work, Plato and Blake. It seems likely that Shaw had read relatively little of Plato – maybe only *The Republic*[10] – but he was someone who could make a little reading go a long way. There can be no doubt that in writing *Man and Superman* he had the Platonic model in mind; the dream in Hell he called 'a Shavio-Socratic dialogue' (CP, II, 503). As the Socratic dialectic led upwards towards the knowledge of the Forms, so Juan's debate with the Devil makes him take the road to a Heaven which is the home of 'the masters of reality'. This is perhaps the significance of a remark of Shaw's quoted in an earlier chapter, describing himself as 'only a realist in the Platonic sense' (CP, I, 483). Shaw's typical method of argument is Socratic in so far as it involves the initial disproof of conventionally held notions of truth to make possible progress towards ultimate philosophic truth. When Juan maintains that the only sort of man who has ever been happy is the philosophic man, he is echoing *The Republic*, and in some sense the Shavian superman is closer to Plato's philosopher king than he is to the Nietzschean *Übermensch*.

Shaw and Plato both believed in the technique of dialectic in the simple meaning of the term – argument through interlocutors as the basic method of truth-seeking. But for Plato there were dimensions of the truth which could not be adequately expressed through the debate of Socrates and his companions, and for these he had recourse to myth and parable. The change of mode from argument to myth in the Platonic dialogue suggests that beyond a certain point it is not possible to convey ultimate realities by direct but only by meta-phoric discourse. Now *Don Juan in Hell* would seem to stand in the same relation to the rest of *Man and Superman* as, say, the myth of Er to *The Republic* or Diotima's parable of the origins and nature of love to *The Symposium*. It is conceived as a level beyond and outside the representational interplay of character and action. But unlike in Plato, it is not a significantly different type of discourse; instead it is merely a purer, more intense form of argumentative debate with Juan taking Tanner's Socratic role. The issues are made more abstract, more fully philosophic in *Don Juan in Hell*, but we never move into the indirect and symbolic mode represented by the

Platonic myth. There is a continuous clarity, very undream-like, in the dream-sequence of *Man and Superman*.

Shaw's incapacity to find a different form of expression is also apparent in *The Revolutionist's Handbook*. We might well expect that a pamphlet written by one of the dramatis personae, a book within the book, would be characteristically by the character rather than by his creator. But *The Revolutionist's Handbook* is just another of Shaw's Prefaces in masquerade – nearly every point made is a familiar Shavian hobby-horse illustrated elsewhere in his work. Perhaps it was as a final attempt to differentiate the *Handbook* from the expository harangue of the Epistle Dedicatory that he added the 'Maxims for Revolutionists'. It is here that Blake comes in. *The Marriage of Heaven and Hell* was clearly a favourite work with Shaw: he cites it as an influence on *The Devil's Disciple* and quotes it in the Epistle Dedicatory to *Man and Superman*. Blake was for him the founding father of the Devil's party, the tradition of nineteenth-century iconoclasm in which he included Ibsen, Nietzsche and no doubt himself.[11] Robert Whitman's claim, therefore, that the 'Maxims for Revolutionists' 'are certainly modelled on and at times echoing Blake's "Proverbs of Hell" ', is no doubt plausible enough.[12] But what a difference between model and imitation. Shaw is scarcely at his best with something as pithy as the maxim anyway; his maxims are always turning into the periods and paragraphs which are his natural stylistic units. Where the maxims do come off, however, it is as satiric epigrams – 'He who can, does. He who cannot, teaches' – and they range in tone from the cynicism of La Rochefoucauld to the flippancy of Wilde. The gnomic enigmatic quality of Blake's aphorisms, or indeed their sheer oddity, are qualities quite foreign to Shaw. The 'Maxims for Revolutionists' are as pointed as everything else in *Man and Superman* and they are frequently the same points.

Part of the difficulty with *Man and Superman* is that there is not enough distinction between Shaw and his two avatars: Shaw *is* Tanner *is* Juan. It seems likely that Shaw did not, in the first instance, model Tanner on himself, in spite of Granville Barker's cultivating recognisably G.B.S. make-up and business in the 1905 production. The introductory description of Tanner, it has been convincingly argued, shows that it was H. M. Hyndman, the Social Democratic orator and agitator, that was in Shaw's mind.[13] Certainly Tanner, with his impulsiveness, his volatility, his all but mad energy, is a realised comic character in the first two acts, not a mere stand-in for Shaw. And Don Juan, although Tanner's alter ego, is distinguished from him: 'A more critical, fastidious, handsome face, paler and colder, without Tanner's impetuous credulity and enthusiasm, and without a touch of his modern plutocratic vulgarity' (CP, II, 632). The distinction is one that is apparent and effective in the theatre for those who have had a chance to see the play in its entirety. But the cooler, more austere Don Juan has in fact shed many of the non-Shavian characteristics of Tanner to become a more formidable spokesman for Shaw. Once the force of the debate takes hold on us, we lose the awareness of his separate identity as Don Juan. We only recognise that he is saying the same things, making the same arguments as Tanner did in Acts I and II, but making them more articulately, more cogently, without Tanner's comic extravagance. As a result we feel that this is what Shaw himself is driving at, through Tanner and through Juan.

Juan is, and is intended to be, more real than Tanner, in Shaw's Platonic sense of the word. With the dream in Hell the stage is cleared of supporting characters, motor-cars and brigands, the inessential props of the main plot, to make way for the 'omnipresent nothing' against which the debate is set. Four voices are enough to argue out the ideological heart of the matter. But after that debate, to return to Tanner and the rest, the Strakers, the Violets and Malones, the cars and the brigands, is to feel that this *is* what Shaw called it, 'a trumpery story of London life'. If in the dream in Hell we sense that we have arrived where Shaw was taking us, the surrounding comedy begins to look like a merely factitious contraption to get us there. The characters of the main plot seem tedious and trivial by contrast with the bravura performers of the dream-sequence. The conventional thickening up of comic complications before the dénouement – the arrival of the Irish-American Malone Senior, the incorporated company of brigands Mendoza Ltd – appear feeble and facetious excrescences.

Act IV is by far the least satisfactory part of *Man and Superman*, to some extent because the comedy looks artificial and contrived once what it was contrived for has been revealed. But it also suffers from the ideological explicitness of the comedy itself. This explicitness seems less obtrusive in the earlier acts of the play. The first love-scene between Ann and Tanner in Act I is amusing because of his ironic lack of awareness of her intentions. There is a comic interplay between his enunciation of his ideas, his account of the development of his moral independence, and the reactions of Ann, hearing only what interests her, seizing any opening to undermine that boasted independence. We laugh at Tanner expatiating on theories of courtship without knowing that he is providing an illustration of his theories himself. The effect in the big scene between Ann and Tanner in Act IV, when he *is* aware of what is happening, is quite different. The combined role of theoretical commentator and unwilling participant then becomes an awkward one. 'We do the world's will, not our own. I have a frightful feeling that I shall let myself be married because it is the world's will that you should have a husband' (CP, II, 725). The awkwardness here is partly a stylistic one; the colloquial lightness of tone in 'I have a frightful feeling that I shall let myself be married' brands as pretentious the talk about the 'world's will'. And yet Shaw believes in the 'world's will' – the whole play has been set up to show its action. There is a similar problem with a joke about the Life Force later on:

> *Ann*: . . . Why are you trying to fascinate me, Jack, if you dont want to marry me?
> *Tanner*: The Life Force. I am in the grip of the Life Force.
> *Ann*: I dont understand in the least: it sounds like the Life Guards.
> (CP, II, 726)

Do we laugh at this, and if so is our laughter directed against Ann's anti-intellectualism or Tanner's pontificating?

It has been argued that in the semi-ironic treatment of Tanner, Shaw was expressing an awareness of his own absurdity, a sceptical acknowledgement of the limitations of his own ideas as applied to the real world.[14] But if that was indeed his aim, the hybrid form of *Man and Superman* makes it impossible for him to bring it off. Comedy is traditionally hostile to theory; a whole category of its butts – the schoolmaster, the pedant, the doctor, the lawyer – are theorists humiliated by the pragmatic force of experience. To some extent Tanner can be aligned with them, and Ann's puncturing attitude towards his grandiose theorising – 'I am so glad you understand politics, Jack: it will be most useful to you if you go into parliament' – is standard comic debunking. But, particularly after the dream in Hell, we are also aware that Shaw believes in Tanner's ideas, however inflatedly he may put them, that they represent as near to Juan's ultimate heavenly reality as it is possible for a limited human character to get. As so often in Shaw's work, the nature of comic truth and the nature of a dialectically established would-be absolute truth are incompatible.

Shaw's explicitness in relation to the comic pattern in *Man and Superman* comes across as a want of artistic tact. Of such tact, a fine example is the reticence of Hippolyta's comment on the midsummer night's dreams, in response to Theseus' speech 'The lunatic, the lover, and the poet':

> But all the story of the night told over,
> And all their minds transfigur'd so together,
> More witnesseth than fancy's images,
> And grows to something of great constancy;
> But, howsoever, strange and admirable.

There is indeed more meaning in the dreams of the lunatic, the lover and the poet than Theseus will allow, but Shakespeare will go no further than hinting with Hippolyta that such meaning exists. The integrity of the self-deprecating form of the midsummer night's dream is preserved from explanation or exegesis. Shaw in *Man and Superman* is not content with showing us the comic pattern, he must explain it as well. The self-consciousness of the interpretation seems embarrassing and out of place, particularly in the context of the final love-scene, if such it may be called. The relationship between Tanner and Ann appears false not because, to quote Judge Brack, 'people don't do things like that', but because in comedy at least, people don't say things like this:

> *Ann*: Well, I made a mistake: you do not love me.
> *Tanner* [*seizing her in his arms*]: It is false: I love you. The Life Force enchants me: I have the whole world in my arms when I clasp you. But I am fighting for my freedom, for my honor, for myself, one and indivisible. (CP, II, 729)

Shaw's habitual difficulty in writing convincing dialogue for his lovers is here increased by his need to expound the significance of their love and love in general.

Man and Superman is an extraordinary *tour de force*. If one has any feeling for Shaw at all, one cannot withold admiration for its inventiveness, its audacity, its combination of skill and stamina. Though in many ways a ramshackle construction, a loose and baggy monster in play-form, it is amazingly ingenious in the integration of its disparate elements. The debate in Hell represents a high-point in Shaw's dramatic rhetoric, so that for all the abstractness of its issues and its apparently static form, it compels concentrated attention in the theatre. Yet locked as it is into its own idiosyncratic form, the whole work seems curiously without resonance and without depth. Its relentless unity of tone and clarity of exposition leave no room for the organic development of form and meaning. It is autonomous, self-validating, remote ultimately from any real experience, even the deliberately distorted experience of comedy. The stereotyped characters of traditional comedy are representatives of universal patterns which implicitly supply significance. Shaw, in making his comic figures articulate their own significance, or rather having John Tanner articulate for all of them, produces an effect of alienating artificiality. *Man and Superman* is in one sense brilliantly successful in marrying comedy with philosophy, but as a work of art it fails ultimately by virtue of its very articulateness.

5 A Geographical Conscience

John Bull's Other Island is the most underrated and neglected of Shaw's major plays. That it is one of his major plays was his own view: it was, he said in 1915 (together with *Man and Superman* and *Major Barbara*), one of 'a group of three plays of exceptional weight and magnitude on which the reputation of the author as a serious dramatist was first established, and still mainly rests' (CP, III, 193). This has been the view, also, of a number of recent critics who have treated it seriously and sympathetically.[1] But many general books on Shaw do not consider it at all, it is infrequently revived and, unlike the bulk of Shaw's plays, it has only recently become available in paperback again, after a lapse of many years. One possible reason for this neglect is a feeling that the play is not only dated but 'placed', that its specific concern with the political and social issues of 1904 Ireland limits its appeal. Certainly all the talk of Home Rule and Land Acts, the local and topical questions of the day, does contribute to this effect. Those critics who have written about the play have not, on the whole, concentrated on its Irishness, but have seen it instead in relation to Shaw's other works: Broadbent, Doyle and Keegan stand for the three elements of the familiar Shavian dialectic;[2] *John Bull* is a development of the pattern of *Candida*, or a prefiguration of the themes of *Major Barbara*.[3] Yet its very anomalousness as the only full-length play Shaw ever set in Ireland, the extent to which as a result it does *not* resemble any of the rest of his work, is perhaps what is most significant and interesting about it.

> John Bull's Other Island was written in 1904 at the request of Mr William Butler Yeats, as a patriotic contribution to the repertory of the Irish Literary Theatre. Like most people who have asked me to write plays, Mr Yeats got rather more than he bargained for. (CP, II, 808)

So Shaw, in the opening sentences of the 'Preface for Politicians', contrived to suggest that *John Bull* was a commissioned work, turned

down by the just-about-to-be Abbey Theatre, and as a result handed
over to Granville Barker at the Royal Court where it was an
enormous success. It was not quite like that. As early as 1900, Shaw
had been considering writing a play 'on the contrast between Irish
and English character' and at that stage Yeats found the idea no
more than 'amusing'.[4] Although at some stage between then and
1904, no doubt Shaw did promise the play to the Irish Literary
Theatre, his letters to Granville Barker through the summer of that
year while he was at work on the play make it clear that it was quite
as definitely promised to the Royal Court, and that its Dublin
production was very much secondary to its London premiere.[5] All
this is significant because we may misread the play if we misconceive
the history of its origins. Shaw declares that 'it was uncongenial to
the whole spirit of the neo-Gaelic movement, which is bent on
creating a new Ireland after its own ideal, whereas my play is a very
uncompromising presentment of the real old Ireland' (CP, II, 808).
But this image of Yeats and the 'neo-Gaelic' idealists rejecting a play
which was too hard-hitting for them does justice neither to Yeats nor
to the play.

In fact Yeats's letter of 'rejection' – for so it has been interpreted
though it by no means rejects the idea of producing the play –
contains a strikingly appreciative and shrewdly perceptive reaction
to *John Bull*:

> I thought in reading the first act that you had forgotten Ireland,
> but I found in the other acts that it is the only subject on which
> you are entirely serious. . . . You have said things in this play
> which are entirely true about Ireland, things which nobody has
> ever said before, and these are the very things that are most part of
> the action. It astonishes me that you should have been so long in
> London and yet have remembered so much. To some extent this
> play is unlike anything you have done before. Hitherto you have
> taken your situations from melodrama, and called up logic to
> make them ridiculous. Your process here seems to be quite
> different, you are taking your situations more from life, you are for
> the first time trying to get the atmosphere of a place, you have for
> the first time a geographical conscience.[6]

Yeats had good reason to be astonished that Shaw should have
remembered Ireland so well. In 1904 it was twenty-eight years since

Shaw had left Dublin and he had never set foot in the country since. (Curiously he returned the following year and thereafter spent many holidays in Ireland.) Yet Rosscullen was entirely authentic – was and to a remarkable extent still is. The Irish setting is indeed realised, as Yeats suggests, in a way that Shaw's earlier plays never are. Whether or not we agree that Ireland is the only subject on which Shaw was really serious, he does have a 'geographical conscience' in *John Bull* and it is this which gives the play its unique character.

The 'Preface for Politicians' and much of the first act of *John Bull* are fairly typically Shavian in object and method. Shaw has as usual certain stock views to combat and he attacks them in his customary way, paradoxically standing them on their heads or letting fire-crackers off under them. Among the stock views on the Irish question which are under assault are theatrical stereotypes, literary ideals and political prejudices. The theatrical stereotype is Shaw's most obvious target, and with Tim Haffigan the native Glaswegian he takes delight in exposing the stage Irishman as a total fake. Doyle berates Broadbent for his credulity:

> Man alive, dont you know that all this top-o-the-morning and broth-of-a-boy and more-power-to-your-elbow business is got up in England to fool you, like the Albert Hall concerts of Irish music? No Irishman ever talks like that in Ireland, or ever did, or ever will. But when a thoroughly worthless Irishman comes to England, and finds the whole place full of romantic duffers like you, who will let him loaf and drink and sponge and brag as long as he flatters your sense of moral superiority by playing the fool and degrading himself and his country, he soon learns the antics that take you in. He picks them up at the theatre or the music hall. (CP, ii, 905–6)

It was this sort of image which the Irish Literary Theatre was founded to combat. 'We shall show', declared the manifesto of 1898, 'that Ireland is not the home of buffoonery and of easy sentiment, as it has been represented, but the home of an ancient idealism.'[7] However Shaw had hardly more time for the 'ancient idealism' than for the 'buffoonery and easy sentiment', and for him the literary ideal of Celticism was no more than an upmarket version of the stage Irishman. When Broadbent burbles on about the 'melancholy of the

Keltic race', Doyle is driven to fury: 'When people talk about the Celtic race, I feel as if I could burn down London. That sort of rot does more harm than ten Coercion Acts' (CP, II, 908).

Though his play was to be concerned with the difference between English and Irish character, and one of his main strategies was to reverse the stereotypes, making the Irishman the hard-headed realist, the Englishman the maudlin sentimentalist, Shaw was unwilling to grant that there were essential racial differences.

> When I say that I am an Irishman I mean that I was born in Ireland, and that my native language is the English of Swift and not the unspeakable jargon of the mid-XIX century London newspapers. My extraction is the extraction of most Englishmen: that is, I have no trace in me of the commercially imported North Spanish strain which passes for aboriginal Irish: I am a genuine typical Irishman of the Danish, Norman, Cromwellian, and (of course) Scotch invasions. (CP, II, 811)

This is directed against separatist nationalism, both cultural and political – the Gaelic League and Sinn Fein. It is because Shaw wishes to insist on the difference between the Irish and the English, yet to deny any racial distinction, that he adopts the preposterous theory that it is climate which makes national character. The 'Preface for Politicians' is full of such preposterous theories but they are all designed to work against currently-held assumptions, often unstated in the Preface itself. For instance, one of the commonest arguments against Home Rule, then and since, was that it would lead to the tyrannical control of Ireland by the Catholic Church and the persecution of the Protestant minority; Home Rule = Rome Rule, as the slogan had it. Shaw sets out to defuse this charge by maintaining (*a*) that the Catholic laity, if given freedom from English rule, would develop a healthy anti-clerical movement, (*b*) the Protestants would find a natural position as forceful and vociferous leaders of a dissenting opposition, (*c*) that the Catholic Church would be less, not more powerful, if it were the established church of the country. Though there is a good deal of perverse Shavian rhetoric in all of this, there is much that is solid and shrewd as well. Shaw's predictions for Ireland under Home Rule were blown off course by Partition and the triumph of the separatism he abhorred, but the evidence of sixty years of an independent Ireland in which the Catholic Church was *not* established – its special status no more than recognised for a time by the Constitution – suggests that his analysis of the power of its independence was valid enough. The 'Preface for Politicians', with its discussion of 'the curse of nationalism', still makes sombrely instructive reading eighty years on.

Larry Doyle is Shaw's spokesman throughout Act I and much of Act III. Larry is given precisely the same arguments in many cases as those advanced by Shaw in the Preface. It is he who argues for an Established Roman Catholic Church, it is he who wants Home Rule as a step towards a Federal Empire in which international standards of social justice may be maintained, it is he who sees the inadequacy of the Land Acts as a settlement of Ireland's problems. Shaw's strategy with Doyle, in the first act particularly, is analogous to his use of Bluntschli in *Arms and the Man*. The formula is to set up a stage soldier/Irishman, a Tim Haffigan or a Sergius, and then to reveal the real soldier/Irishman, Bluntschli or Larry Doyle, as the direct opposite. Yet the technique comes out very differently in *John Bull* because the reality of Larry as real Irishman takes Shaw into a quite different emotional range. The comic effect of Bluntschli is his prosaic matter-of-factness, his imperturbability, showing up the inflated emotions of military romance by contrast. When Sergius ends the play with his famous exclamation 'What a man! Is he a man!', the doubt is to some extent the audience's too. Bluntschli is less a man than a marvellous comic device, himself by definition neutral and unchanging. In *John Bull*, however, Shaw not only uses Larry to expose and explode the stage-Irishman and myths about the Celtic race, he reveals also the motives that lead Larry to expose and explode. And they are very mixed motives.

There is an unnecessary acrimony in Doyle's denunciation of Tim Haffigan; Broadbent, who is not stupid humanly in relation to his partner if in nearly everything else, notices it: 'What's wrong with you today, Larry? Why are you so bitter? (CP, II, 906). It turns out that a number of things are wrong with Larry, all of them centring on thoughts of his native Rosscullen. He has been upset by Broadbent's news:

> Your foreclosing this Rosscullen mortgage and turning poor Nick Lestrange out of house and home has rather taken me aback; for I liked the old rascal when I was a boy and had the run of his park to play in. I was brought up on the property. (CP, II, 906)

Doyle was the son of Nick Lestrange's land-agent, as it later emerges, and the dispossession of the traditional occupant of the property stirs uncomfortably old feelings of loyalty. Yet this is only part of the trouble. The foreclosing of the mortgage necessarily will mean business involvement with the estate, and therefore a return to Rosscullen which Larry dreads. 'I have an instinct against going back to Ireland: an instinct so strong that I'd rather go with you to the South Pole than to Rosscullen' (CP, II, 907). He holds forth at length on the nature of Ireland and the Irish experience which makes him so reluctant to return, until Broadbent pulls him up short by spotting a more specific source of reluctance:

> a moment ago I caught a name which is new to me: a Miss Nora Reilly, I think. . . . I dont wish to be impertinent, as you know, Larry; but are you sure she has nothing to do with your reluctance to come to Ireland with me? (CP, II, 915)

Yet Larry's feeling of guilt about Nora, although it is the feeling which he was not altogether confessing to himself, is not pinpointed as the real or ultimate source of his disquiet, making the others invalid excuses. Everything he has said works together to make a complex network in which each strand contributes to the over-all pattern of emotional ambiguity and uncertainty.

Larry Doyle is unique among Shaw's characters in displaying this particular sort of complexity. On the whole Shaw's characterisation is the relatively stable characterisation of comedy. His people are what they are; if they change, they change suddenly and completely under the trauma of disillusionment – Harry Trench, Vivie Warren, Major Barbara – or by conversion – Dick Dudgeon, Captain Brassbound, Blanco Posnet. This is not to say his characters are flat rather than round. That distinction, if it has any value, has value only for the characters of the realistic novel to which it was first applied. Dramatic figures can convince us entirely of their reality for two hours on the stage without showing a capacity for change or development, particularly in comedy where change or development are unusual. In *John Bull*, in fact, as Shaw himself was quick to observe, the character of Larry Doyle tends to be overshadowed theatrically by Broadbent, the comic star of the show, and Keegan the dramatic star. The distinctiveness of Doyle is that, like a character in Ibsen or Chekhov, and unlike most of Shaw's, he gives the impression of having an inner life to which his words and actions only testify obliquely. In Shaw normally the characters tell us all we need to know, or if they do not Shaw does; there is only text, no sub-text. But with Larry, at crucial moments, we have to guess at the truth. What, if anything, does he really feel for Nora? Shaw's stage direction assures us that he is 'quite unconscious of his cruelty' to her in the dreadful non-event of their first talk together alone in Act IV, but how unconscious is he? His later apology suggests that his nonchalance was affected: 'When I left you that time, I was just as wretched as you. I didnt rightly know what I wanted to say; and my tongue kept clacking to cover the loss I was at' (CP, II, 1008). In the meantime Nora has got engaged to Broadbent, as she reveals to him bitterly and triumphantly. What are we to make of his reply?

> *Larry* [*naïvely*]: But that was the very thing I was going to advise you to do. (CP, II, 1008)

Whether we accept that this is naïve, or a cynical mask for a sense of shock, there is a real question for an actor playing Larry as to the motives behind the part, as there rarely is for actors in other Shaw parts.

Larry occupies this unusual position among Shaw's characters because he and his feelings about Ireland stand in an unusually close relation to Shaw himself. Shaw, like Larry, is impatient with generalisations about the Celtic race. The passage most often quoted from Larry's great 'dreaming' speech in Act I is Shaw's jibe at the sentimental nationalist rhetoric of Yeats among others. The Irishman, we are told,

> cant be intelligently political: he dreams of what the Shan Van Vocht said in ninety-eight. If you want to interest him in Ireland youve got to call the unfortunate island Kathleen ni Houlihan and pretend she's a little old woman. (CP, II, 910)

Yet what is the speech but an analysis of the Celtic life of the imagination:

> Oh, the dreaming! the dreaming! the torturing, heart-scalding, never satisfying dreaming, dreaming, dreaming, dreaming! [*Savagely*] No debauchery that ever coarsened and brutalised an Englishman can take the worth and usefulness out of him like that dreaming. An Irishman's imagination never lets him alone, never

convinces him, never satisfies him; but it makes him that he cant face reality nor deal with it nor handle it nor conquer it: he can only sneer at them that do. (CP, II, 909)

This is not to disagree with the Matthew Arnold idea of the Celts as dreamers not doers,[8] but to dissent from the view of the Celtic Revivalists that this is reason for self-congratulation. What is significant in the speech is the series of stage directions indicating the tone in which it is spoken: 'savagely', 'bitterly', 'with fierce, shivering self-contempt'. This is not a satiric Shavian diatribe against Irish myth-mongering; it is a bitter national self-analysis.

Shaw is speaking especially personally through Larry in the peroration of the speech where he moves on to the mockery which is the complement of the Irishman's dreaming:

[*Dropping his voice like a man making some shameful confidence*] And all the while there goes on a horrible, senseless, mischievous laughter. When youre young, you exchange vile stories with them; and as youre too futile to be able to help or cheer them, you chaff and sneer and taunt them for not doing the things you darent do yourself. And all the time you laugh! laugh! laugh! eternal derision, eternal envy, eternal folly, eternal fouling and staining and degrading, until, when you come at last to a country where men take a question seriously and give a serious answer to it, you deride them for having no sense of humor, and plume yourself on your own worthlessness as if it made you better than them. (CP, II, 910–11)

This is echoed in Shaw's fierce comment on *Ulysses* as the portrait of 'a disgusting phase of civilisation; but . . . a truthful one'.

I should like to put a cordon round Dublin; round up every male person in it between the ages of 15 and 30; force them to read it; and ask them whether on reflection they could see anything amusing in all that foul-mouthed, foul-minded derision and obscenity.[9]

Shaw's Puritanism speaks through this, but also his hatred of the cynical belittling laughter of Dublin, the laughter of Buck Mulligan. There can be no doubt that for Shaw as for Larry, England was the 'country where men take a question seriously and give a serious answer to it', and immensely to be preferred to Ireland for that reason. Doyle's partnership with Broadbent, based on a mixture of affectionate contempt, real respect, and even love, is a curious metaphor for Shaw's relationship with the English. All his life Shaw used his Irishness as a vantage-point to tease, scold, denounce and mock the English, frequently 'deriding them for having no sense of humor'. But England was the real workaday world for all that, and the adult Shaw never wanted to live anywhere else. Its solidity, even its humourlessness, were a reassurance against the cycle of dream and disillusion of Larry's speech.

Larry Doyle is the most subtle study of the emotions of the Irish exile before Joyce – the dream of escape and the fear of return, the guilty shame and self-disgust of nationality. Though he is given Shavian views on ways to improve Ireland socially and politically, at a deeper level he is driven to destroy Rosscullen to justify his own desertion and betrayal of it. When he foretells the triumph of the syndicate in 'developing' the area, he glories vindictively and desperately in its ruthlessness. He can feel that he has allied himself with the unstoppable force of big business so that he both is and is not responsible for the commercial rape of his own country. (Broadbent has to remind him that he has shares in the syndicate too.) In all of this Larry is certainly not very like a self-portrait of Shaw. The Roman Catholic civil engineer, son of a small country land-agent, is not an obvious mask for Shaw, the journalist-turned-playwright from a Dublin background of down-at-heel Protestant ascendancy. And yet the success of Larry Doyle seems to me to derive from the projection into a figure safely unlike himself of very real feelings of his own. As W. R. Beard put it, in a useful dissertation on *John Bull*: 'Shaw was always fond of quoting the Biblical saying that "the heart only knows its own bitterness". In Larry Doyle he attempted to give dramatic expression to his heart's bitterness.'[10]

However it was not only the part of Larry Doyle that Shaw created, but the whole of the play. If in Doyle he found expression for some of his deepest and most unhappy feelings about nationality, he did not cheat us of a very funny comedy about the differences between English and Irish character. *John Bull* was a popular if not a critical success at its first production, culminating in the famous royal command performance at which the King broke the specially provided royal chair with laughing. The reviewers complained of the play's plotlessness, its lack of construction, but the real glory of *John Bull* is the freewheeling comedy which arises from turning

Broadbent loose in Ireland. Shaw revenged generations of Teagues and Paddies when he created Tom Broadbent, the stage Englishman. No stage-Irish buffoonery could be more extravagant or more fantastic that the show Broadbent puts on for Rosscullen. His tourist-book enthusiasm –

> *Broadbent*: . . . Just a moment, Mr Doyle: I want to look at this stone. It must be Finian's die-cast.
> *Cornelius* [*in blank bewilderment*]: Hwat? (CP, II, 932)

his blithering sentimentalism, his political rhetoric make him for the Irish a zany figure of fun. The reaction after his address to the 'electoral committee' in Act III is typical:

> *Father Dempsey* [*indulgently*]: Well, he hasnt much sense, God help him. (CP, II, 970)

It is one of Shaw's most brilliant comic strokes to show in the Irish attitude to the English precisely that air of complacent patronage which underlies the traditional English reception of the stage Irishman.

The extravagant antics of Broadbent are seen from the viewpoint of the realities of Rosscullen. Although the play may have been an initial success in London, much of its comedy is more accessible to an Irish audience because it requires familiarity with the nuances of Irish life to appreciate Broadbent's absurd ignorance of them. His confusion about tea and dinner, his expectation of finding a bed for the night in a Rosscullen public-house, his mispronunciation of Irish names which makes Nora laugh even in the midst of her heartbreak, are all funnier if one does not have to rely on Shaw's explanations of them in the stage directions. Yeats was surely right to wonder that Shaw had 'remembered so much' in creating Rosscullen. The social details of class hierarchy are meticulously observed: the gulf between the landless labourer, Patsy Farrell, and even the smallest of small farmers, Matt Haffigan; the absolute horror of Nora, the 'heiress' to £ 40 a year, at having been made to shake hands with Doolan the publican in the main street of Rosscullen and the still greater horror at being sent to call on Doolan's wife; the alliance of the 'men of substance', Corny Doyle, Matt Haffigan, Barny Doran, with Father Dempsey in selecting the parliamentary candidate. The Doyle household, with Aunt Judy the sister/housekeeper, and Nora who came on a visit when she was seventeen and stayed ever since, is created with equal accuracy. One can watch Broadbent cringe with horrified embarrassment, for example, at the basic domesticity revealed in Aunt Judy's unselfconscious offer of hospitality: 'Come! is it the sofa youre afraid of? If it is, you can have me own bed. I can sleep with Nora' (CP, II, 936). Shaw himself was Dublin born and bred, but there is a piercing truth about his portrait of small town and country Ireland.

Yet for all Larry Doyle's fierce debunking and the steady realism of Shaw's picture of Rosscullen, the first view of Ireland we are given is of a highly romantic figure in a highly romantic landscape.

> Rosscullen. Westward a hillside of granite rock and heather slopes upward across the prospect from south to north. A huge stone stands on it in a naturally impossible place, as if it had been tossed up there by a giant. Over the brow, in the desolate valley beyond, is a round tower. A lonely white high road trending away westward past the tower loses itself at the foot of the far mountains. It is evening; and there are great breadths of silken green in the Irish sky. The sun is setting.
>
> A man with the face of a young saint, yet with white hair and perhaps 50 years on his back, is standing near the stone in a trance of intense melancholy, looking over the hills as if by mere intensity of gaze he could pierce the glories of the sunset and see into the streets of heaven. (CP, II, 922)

This is as sentimentally picturesque as a Moore's Melody; one can all but hear the harp. Essential to the design of the play is the strongest possible contrast between Broadbent and Doyle, seen in the first act in their London office, and Peter Keegan. To enforce this contrast Shaw took the bold theatrical risk of opening Act II with the conversation between Keegan and the grasshopper. It is a scene on the edge of a shudderingly arch whimsicality, perhaps right over the edge. (Interestingly Synge, who read the play in manuscript, thought it should be cut.)[11] Yet it involves a theatrical strategy which can be made to work with a good enough actor, because of the convincing modulation of Irish voice and persona which it and the succeeding scenes involve. The brogue which Keegan uses in this opening scene, Shaw tells us, 'is the jocular assumption of a gentleman and not the natural speech of a peasant' (CP, II, 922). The original London audience, however, would not have had the benefit of such a direction and might well have taken the stage Irish speech which Keegan here mimics for the real thing. If so, they would have heard a contrast when he talks to Patsy Farrell – for whom the fantasy conversation with the grasshopper seems only too real. His language here is quite different, without the stock locutions of stage Irish: 'An is that yourself,' 'Sure it's the wise grasshopper yar.' And yet, like many educated Irish people talking to the less educated, he uses something like the idiom and pronunciation of Patsy himself: 'Is that your religion, to be afraid of a little deeshy grasshopper? Suppose it was a divil, what call have you to fear it?' (CP, II, 925). This again changes when Keegan meets Nora Reilly and he drops 'the broad Irish vernacular of his speech to Patsy'. From the fantastic eccentricity of the grasshopper scene Keegan is moved towards a realistic social persona by this shifting pattern of speech.

Keegan is the first of Shaw's mystics, the figures in his work whom he used to express a vision transcending that of the more obviously Shavian rationalists. He has been most often, and rightly, compared with Captain Shotover. But Shotover's crazed vision is compromised by the craziness of all the other denizens of *Heartbreak House*. He is inclined to appear no more than one more oddball in that collection of oddities. Keegan, though a symbolic voice like Shotover, is seen in relation to a very ordinary and very real social scene. He is the unfrocked parish priest of Rosscullen, regarded with some jealous hostility by his successor Father Dempsey, treated respectfully by people like the Doyles and Nora Reilly, winning an admiring awe from the villagers which gives him some involuntary political influence. He is peripheral to the life of Rosscullen, but of it none the less. The story of how the black man put a spell on him and drove him mad is very much like the selling of Captain Shotover's soul to the devil in Zanzibar. But with Keegan, when we get the truth, it is a sobering and moving story in which we can quite simply believe.

The doctrine revealed to Keegan by the death-bed confession of the Hindu is that the earth itself is Hell, a place of torment to which human beings are sent for crimes committed in a former existence. Shaw's use of this concept of Hell is extraordinarily unlike that in *Man and Superman*. The dream-debate in *Man and Superman* took place in 'omnipresent nothing'; Hell was simply a void in which people talked. Shaw mocked the literalist idea of an actual place of torment, and indeed argued that for the damned the Inferno is a place of pleasure. The Hell of *Man and Superman* starts as a joke and retains something of the joke throughout. By contrast Peter Keegan's Hell is the here and now, the world, Ireland, Rosscullen. His doctrine is the more telling for the very ordinariness of the life which he sees as hellish. Life without purpose was for Shaw a state of damnation, as he made clear in *Man and Superman*; but there the idea was only an idea, the statement of a principle. The purposelessness of the lives of Nora Reilly and Corny Doyle, of Barney Doran and Matt Haffigan, is bleakly realised. Shaw's truth to the experience of a particular time and place – what Yeats called his geographical conscience – lends substance to Keegan's anguished revulsion from the human world which he sees.

Keegan's presence, believing what he does, is intended to sour and subvert the comedy, particularly in the final act. The third act moves to an expectant ending, with the prospect of Broadbent taking Haffigan's pig home in the motor-car clearly planned as a comic *pièce de resistance*. Act IV opens just as we might expect, with the story of that misadventure in all its glorious detail. But Shaw alters the expected perspective by making 'Keegan the central figure in a rather crowded apartment' (CP, II, 979). The group surrounding Barney Doran, now on his fourth telling of the tale of the pig, is off-centre. Shaw made clear in a letter to the actor William Poel, who was to play Keegan in a revival of *John Bull*, just the effect he planned:

> Keegan plays a very important part silently in the atrocious scene of the recital of the pig story by Doran. It is his presence that keeps the scene human. He really feels in hell. And I need not tell you that the effect is very mixed; for the audience are caught one way by the infection of Doran's barbarous fun (which they also foolishly think the proper Irish thing) and are consequently as much rebuked by Keegan's attitude as the laughers on the stage. (CL, II, 642)

Shaw's personal hatred for cruelty to animals and his abhorrence of the derisive laughter which he thought of as specifically Irish weights the scene for him towards Keegan, and there may be some danger that the less sensitive among an audience might laugh on with Doran regardless. The story is, after all, a very funny one. But the effect of Keegan's silent presence is, at least, to make us guilty about our laughter.

The account of the pig is only the most spectacular instance of Keegan's challenge to the comic. It is not until Act IV that we see Broadbent and Doyle on stage with Keegan, but when we do their comic partnership, which worked so splendidly in Act I, ceases to seem so funny. The comedy of Broadbent is essentially that of bathos. His response to Larry's great 'dreaming' speech is a good example:

> *Broadbent* [*roused to intense earnestness by Doyle's eloquence*] : Never despair, Larry. There are great possibilities for Ireland. Home Rule will work wonders under English guidance. (CP, II, 911)

Our laughter at Broadbent derives always from something close to embarrassment, the embarrassment of watching someone sublimely unaware of his lack of understanding. In the presence of Keegan what has been marvellously comic, even likeable in Broadbent, begins to seem merely embarrassing. His Philistine optimism is fatuous rather than funny juxtaposed with Keegan's tragic vision:

> *Keegan*: You feel at home in the world, then?
> *Broadbent*: Of course. Dont you?
> *Keegan* [*from the very depths of his nature*] : No.
> *Broadbent* [*breezily*] : Try phosphorus pills. I always take them when my brain is overworked. I'll give you the address in Oxford Street. (CP, II, 992)

This might be just a bad or misplaced joke on Shaw's part, but it seems more likely that we wince because we are intended to wince. The unfunniness of Broadbent in the last act is part of a general revaluation of Broadbent and Doyle in which Keegan is the main agent. We see here, in part through Keegan's (unlikely) fore-knowledge of the syndicate's financial manoeuvres, that for all the Englishman's absurdity, he will be devastatingly, even sinisterly efficient in his 'development' of Rosscullen. Larry Doyle's bitter mixed feelings about Ireland with which we sympathised in Act I, become finally a convulsive self-hatred, vented in an aggressive hostility to Keegan who represents a level of understanding which he resents as a reproach to himself.

The sharpest exchange between Keegan and Doyle has striking implications for the meaning of the play as a whole.

Keegan: In the accounts kept in heaven, Mr Doyle, a heart
purified of hatred may be worth more than even a Land
Development Syndicate of Anglicized Irishmen and
Gladstonized Englishmen.

Larry: Oh, in heaven, no doubt. I have never been there. Can you
tell me where it is?

Keegan: Could you have told me this morning where hell is? Yet
you know now that it is here. Do not despair of finding heaven:
it may be no further off.

Larry [*ironically*] : On this holy ground, as you call it, eh?

Keegan [*with fierce intensity*] : Yes, perhaps, even on this holy ground
which such Irishmen as you have turned into a Land of
Derision. (CP, II, 1019)

For all that Keegan goes on to assert that 'my country is not Ireland
nor England, but the whole mighty realm of my Church', there is
surely special significance in the emphasis on Ireland as holy
ground. Earlier he expanded on this theme to Broadbent:

Ireland, sir, for good or evil, is like no other place under heaven;
and no man can touch its sod or breathe its air without becoming
better or worse. It produces two kinds of men in strange
perfection: saints and traitors. It is called the island of saints; but
indeed in these later years it might be more fitly called the island
of the traitors; for our harvest of these is the fine flower of the
world's crop of infamy. But the day may come when these islands
shall live by the quality of their men rather than by the
abundance of their minerals; and then we shall see. (CP, II, 1016)

Doyle, who had wanted Ireland to provide the brains and
imagination of a federal commonwealth of nations, in the context of
this final scene seems more like one of Ireland's traitors. Shaw,
apparently so much in accordance with Doyle's views in the earlier
part of the play, here seems to throw his weight behind Keegan's
national messianism. ' "The island of saints" ', he remarks in the
Preface for Politicians, 'is no idle phrase. Religious genius is one of
our national products; Ireland is no bad rock to build a Church on'
(CP, II, 837). One of the paradoxes of *John Bull* is that in some sense
it could well have been what Shaw called it with apparent irony, 'a
patriotic contribution to the repertory of the Irish Literary Theatre'.

The play is not merely 'a very uncompromising presentment of the real old Ireland'. It contains the suggestion of a new and holy Ireland, different no doubt from Yeats's ideal of a nation restored to Unity of Culture, but not all that different – 'a country in which the State is the Church and the Church the people: three in one and one in three' (CP, II, 1021).

'Father Keegan is one of Shaw's most arresting creations, and his characterisation reveals Shaw's mastery in depicting the religious temperament.'[12] With this I cannot altogether agree. For all the boldness of the imaginative conception of Keegan, his religious vision does not seem to me finally authentic or convincing. This is partly because of a selfconscious knowingness in his role as wise madman. 'My way of joking is to tell the truth,' he says portentously. 'It's the funniest joke in the world' (CP, II, 930). Keegan is most obviously Shaw's spokesman when he stresses the significance of the apparently fantastic: 'Every dream is a prophecy: every jest is an earnest in the womb of Time' (CP, II, 1021). There is a covert belief in an idea of progress here, Shaw's faith that, given time enough, man moves towards perfection, and that jesters like himself, 'madmen' like Keegan, are the seers of that future. This comes out as a sort of transcendental rationalism rather than the irrationalism it claims to be, a vision not of the mystic whose experience is out of time, but of the unusually far-sighted. Keegan gives us a Trinity shorn of mystery and the supernatural. This is his version of Heaven as against Broadbent's 'pale blue satin place':[13]

> In my dreams it is a country where the State is the Church and the Church the people: three in one and one in three. It is a commonwealth in which work is play and play is life: three in one and one in three. It is a temple in which the priest is the worshipper and the worshipper the worshipped: three in one and one in three. It is a godhead in which all life is human and all humanity divine: three in one and one in three. It is, in short, the dream of a madman. (CP, II, 1021)

But to secularise the Trinity is to deny its meaning, and the impression left by this final speech of Keegan's, for all its rhetorical afflatus, is of a rather thin humanism.

What is moving in *John Bull* is not so much the character of Keegan as that Shaw should have felt the need to create him. *John Bull* is the one play, Larry Doyle the one character, in which Shaw revealed the emotional background out of which he created the persona of G.B.S, the tireless, changeless public figure, Yeats's 'sewing-machine that smiled'. Without *John Bull*, one would be much more inclined to accept Yeats's image as the truth about Shaw. In Larry Doyle Shaw faced the feelings of provinciality, of divided national identity, of emotional instability which confirmed him an Irish exile. But he also faced the self-destructiveness implicit in that aggressive rejection of Ireland. And to transcend Doyle he created Keegan. As a result there is a pressure of feeling in *John Bull*, both in Doyle and Keegan, that is not to be found elsewhere in Shaw's work. Keegan's Utopian vision may be less than adequate, but his denunciation of present evils has the fierce ring of conviction: 'For four wicked centuries the world has dreamed this foolish dream of efficiency; and the end is not yet. But the end will come' (CP, II, 1018). Shaw himself, like Larry Doyle, was again and again driven to the worship of efficiency out of impatience with the aimlessness of idealism, never more strikingly than in his next play, *Major Barbara*. But in *John Bull* efficiency is the gospel of Broadbent rather than Undershaft, and it is placed as wicked illusion by Keegan. The reality of Ireland both social and spiritual, the ambiguous attitudes which it evokes in the several characters, gives *John Bull* its emotional range and complexity. Max Beerbohm's appreciative review of its first production still seems to me to hit the mark:

> I think that none of Mr Shaw's plays has so much serious interest. From all his plays one derives the pleasure that there is in finding a playwright who knows, and gives us, something of the world at first hand – a playwright who, moreover, has a philosophic view of things, and can criticise what he sees. Such displeasure as we have in Mr Shaw's plays comes from the sense that Mr Shaw is a little too sure of himself and his philosophy – a little too loudly consistent about everything to be right about most things. In this latest play of his, he seems to have mellowed into something almost like dubiety, without losing anything of his genius for ratiocination.[14]

6 Giving the Devil More Than His Due

Major Barbara is of central significance in Shaw's work. It recapitulates themes and techniques of many of the earlier plays in an imaginative dramatic structure all its own. Like the Unpleasant plays, *Widowers' Houses* and *Mrs Warren's Profession*, it is concerned with uncovering the economic facts which lie beneath the social surfaces of capitalism. Barbara, like Harry Trench and Vivie Warren, is given a disillusioning education in the workings of the cash nexus. As in the *Plays for Puritans*, *The Devil's Disciple* and *Captain Brassbound*, Shaw's theme is conversion; not only the conversions which Barbara attempts in the Salvation Army shelter, but the conversion of her and Cusins which Undershaft effects in the munitions works at Perivale St Andrews. But *Major Barbara* has also the wider and deeper ideological concerns of the two major plays which immediately preceded it and to which it is linked, *Man and Superman* and *John Bull's Other Island*. In the conflict between the religion of the Salvation Army and Undershaft's religion of money and gunpowder Shaw found a new and arresting vehicle for his most fundamental intellectual and spiritual themes. *Major Barbara* is his fullest attempt to ask and answer the question – what then must we do to be saved?

As so often Shaw begins with the invincibly ignorant, those who have never asked themselves the question, or are unaware that there is a question to be asked. The play opens in the pleasant surroundings of Wilton Crescent with the egregious Stephen and his mother Lady Britomart. Lady Brit was apparently modelled on the Countess of Carlisle, the mother-in-law of Gilbert Murray, the original of Adolphus Cusins, and it has been argued that Shaw exploited in her what he found in her real-life counterpart, a paradoxical contrast between libertarian Whig principles and personal despotism.[1] But it is hard to see Lady Brit as having very significant political views at all. Though we are told that she is 'quite enlightened and liberal as to the books in the library, the pictures on the walls, the music in the portfolios, and the articles in the papers', Shaw takes no trouble with her, as he did for instance with Roebuck Ramsden, to establish a theoretically progressive political position to undermine satirically. As the managing aristocratic matron, hers is a nearly pure comic character part, more humanly realised than Wilde's Lady Bracknell, to whom she is related, but only just.

Stephen, Lady Britomart, even the near Wodehousian Charles Lomax, represent an unquestioned belief in a social, moral and religious *status quo*:

> *Stephen*: . . . Right is right; and wrong is wrong; and if a man cannot distinguish them properly, he is either a fool or a rascal; thats all.
> *Lady Britomart* [*touched*] : Thats my own boy. (CP, III, 76)

Lomax belongs to the Established Church because it is bad form to be a dissenter. The religion of Wilton Crescent, in so far as it has one, is a religion of social conformism. For Lady Brit breezy informality is inappropriate for sacred subjects. If there is to be an impromptu service, 'I insist on having it in a proper and respectable way. Charles: ring for prayers' (CP, III, 91–2). But the dissenters, with 'Onward Christian Soldiers' on the concertina and tambourine, win the day against the social rite of family prayers, and Lady Brit herself is drawn away leaving Stephen alone clinging to his dignity on a deserted stage.

Shaw treats the conformists in *Major Barbara* with comic indulgence. Lady Britomart and Charles Lomax are caricatures, but not satiric caricatures. Only Stephen, the complacent would-be politician who knows nothing but the difference between right and wrong, is treated with less than generosity. Shaw has a comedian's affection for his comic characters and employs them throughout the play for diversion and entertainment. He refuses to take seriously at all the conventional attitudes they represent: Stephen's cherished belief in political democracy; Lady Britomart's trust in blue blood and aristocratic leadership; Lomax's inane orthodoxy – 'I have never shut my eyes to the fact that there is a certain amount of tosh about the Salvation Army' (CP, III, 140). Shaw can afford to laugh and let us laugh at these because they are of no real interest to him. From early on it is apparent that the characters who matter in the play's dialectic are the radical dissenters, Barbara, Cusins and Undershaft.

The first act of *Major Barbara* is designed to set up the terms for the
great debate which follows and the exchange of visits – Undershaft
to the Salvation Army shelter, Barbara to the munitions works –
which gives the debate its theatrical shape. It provides also a norm
of prosperous upper-class life against which the poverty of West
Ham comes as a calculated shock. Shaw points the contrast between
the life of the rich and the poor by his comments on Rummy
Mitchens and Snobby Price's reaction to the cold:

> If they were rich people, gloved and muffed and well wrapped up
> in furs and overcoats, they would be numbed and miserable; for it
> is a grindingly cold raw January day; and a glance at the
> background of grimy warehouses and leaden sky visible over the
> whitewashed walls of the yard would drive any idle rich person
> straight to the Mediterranean. But these two, being no more
> troubled with visions of the Mediterranean than of the moon, and
> being compelled to keep more of their clothes in the pawnshop,
> and less on their persons, in winter than in summer, are not
> depressed by the cold: rather are they stung into vivacity. (CP, III,
> 95–6)

The family conclave was assembled in Act I to see that the
Undershaft daughters and sons-in-law were provided with an
adequate income. Barbara and Sarah could not possibly be
supported on £800 a year, and they can expect no help from their
grandfather, the Earl of Stevenage, whose annual income is a mere
£7000. In the Salvation Army shelter we meet Peter Shirley, a
fitter, starving at the age of forty-five because he has been declared
too old for the job which he had done for the previous ten years. Or
there is Bill Walker who offers Jenny Hill a pound as indemnity for
hitting her – half his savings for the winter. Major Barbara herself
who, we were told in the first act, had dismissed her maid and lived
on £1 a week, works desperately to raise the street collection up to
five shillings. For those of us who have grown up in the British Isles
since social welfare benefits and redundancy payments have become
relatively normal, there is a real dramatic impact in Shaw's
evocation of Disraeli's two nations, still as far apart as ever in the
reign of Edward VII.

When it was rumoured that Shaw was writing a play about the
Salvation Army, the supposition was that it would be a satire. This
idea Shaw indignantly rejected. If nothing else, the fact that the

Salvation Army recognised the appalling poverty in their society and were concerned to help the poor would have won his respect. But there were other features of the Army which genuinely attracted him. The militant image of the soldiers of Christ fighting against His enemies with tambourine and drum appealed to him as the very opposite of the suffering Crosstianity which he opposed. Shaw, the dramatist of the cart and the trumpet, delighted in the razzmatazz of the Army's public meetings. The very fact that it was 'bad form' for the likes of Charles Lomax, its enthusiasm embarrassing and vulgar, was an added reason for Shaw to support it. But at a deeper level the evangelism of the Salvationists matched Shaw's own sense of mission. Their radical and undoctrinaire form of Christianity, with its emphasis on the truth of the individual spirit, was likely to mean more to him than more orthodox Christian cults.

And yet it is, of course, true – though Shaw tried to deny it in the Preface to *Major Barbara* – that the object of the second act is to make us question the activities of the Salvation Army, or any other philanthropic agency in an unjust capitalist society. From the start Shaw plants sceptical witnesses among the clients of the West Ham shelter. Snobby Price and Rummy Mitchens evoke between them the uses and abuses of the public confession. Snobby, the cynical good-for-nothing, is going to work up a story of beating his old mother, knowing that it is this sort of shock-effect which the Salvation Army welcomes. The more spectacularly wicked the past, the more spectacular the conversion, the better the collection at the meeting. 'Oh Snobby', says Barbara, 'if you had given your poor mother just one more kick, we should have got the whole five shillings!' (CP, III, 123). The expected punch-line comes when Snobby has to run in terror: 'your mother's askin for you at the other gate in Cripps' Lane. She's heard about your confession' (CP, III, 129). Rummy, who feels that she owes it to the kindly Salvation Army girls to give them the sort of lurid confession they expect, complains to Snobby: 'you men can tell your lies right out at the meetins and be made much of for it; while the sort of confessions we az to make az to be wispered to one lady at a time' (CP, III, 98).

However well-intentioned the Salvation Army may be, the cash facts underlie and distort all that it does. Those who come to the Army in need know that they cannot expect to have something for nothing. For bread and treacle, they pay in fake sensational confessions and the hypocritical cant of religious enthusiasm. With this sort of barter Shaw prepares the way for the revelation of how easily the Army itself may be bought by its arch-enemies Bodger and Undershaft. Yet the religion offered by the Army in *Major Barbara* is not merely Marx's opium of the people. Undershaft does make the telling point that the Salvation Army helps to draw the teeth of the poor, that as an employer of labour he approves of it as it distracts workers from their grievances. But Shaw does not press home the point; the Salvation Army as we see it in action in Act II is not merely an involuntary agent of capitalism teaching the poor to accept the system rather than revolt against it – Brecht's view of it in *Happy End* or *Saint Joan of the Stockyards*. Though Snobby Price and Rummy Mitchens may be witnesses to the element of hypocritical playacting in the Salvation Army's mission, the incident of Bill Walker is intended to show us that it has real purpose and meaning.

Barbara's near conversion of Bill is a simple illustration of what Shaw understood by Christianity. What is crucial is the refusal to meet aggression with aggression, to fall in with the expected pattern of crime and punishment. Barbara will not accept Bill's various attempts to atone for his attack on Jenny Hill, neither his willingness to take a beating himself nor his offer of money. Her attitude is distinguished from that of Jenny who is more conventionally Christian, praying for Bill and proclaiming her forgiveness of him. Shaw was inclined to dislike and distrust the emotional attitude of turning the other cheek, the whole Christian ethic of suffering and self-abnegation. Instead what he admires and offers as exemplary in Barbara is a neutral self-possession which totally disconcerts Bill, used only to bully or be bullied. The key directions are 'quite sunny and fearless', 'with a gentle voice that never lets him go'. Barbara releases the power of conscience in Bill by letting him see the thug that he is, but responding to him without either the fear or the hatred due to thugs. Again and again she throws him by simply side-stepping the force of his own aggressive momentum. This is Shaw's interpretation of the Chrisian injunction to return evil with good. It is not a matter of loving one's enemies in any very emotional sense; that for Shaw was suspect because partly masochistic. It is rather the ability not to regard one's enemy as alien, simply to recognise his or her existence as a human individual. It is this which Bill Walker finds so bewildering and which so nearly brings about his conversion.

Shaw is aware, and makes us aware, that Barbara's success as a Salvationist derives from her class-based habit of authority. She is her managing mother's daughter, every inch a major, and Bill

Walker is inclined to be in awe of her from the start. But this does not lessen her achievement in Shaw's eyes. We will her on in her wooing of Bill; we share in the bitterness of her defeat. The whole of the second act builds towards that defeat, which has little or no effect if we have not participated in the near success which precedes it. It is the work of salvation which is crucial to Barbara not the business of poor relief and the really devastating effect of her father's gift to the Army is the way in which it destroys the meaning of her mission. What hurts most is Bill Walker's triumphant cry, 'Wot prawce selvytion nah?' Salvation has its price, it cannot be achieved without money any more than any other human activity. That is the materialist message of the second act of *Major Barbara*. But it is enforced with a degree of sympathy and respect for the task of salvation which makes of the climax a real moment of painful human drama, not merely a complacent socio-economic demonstration.

Through most of his visit to the Salvation Army shelter, Undershaft plays a waiting-game, voicing his scepticism only to Cusins, making no direct attempt to question what Barbara is doing. The centre stage is left to the conversion of Bill Walker. It is only when Mrs Baines, the Salvation Army Commissioner, appears that Undershaft sees his chance. He 'pricks up his ears' at the name of the heaven-sent new benefactor of the Army, and takes a malicious pleasure in disclosing how the distiller Horace Bodger became the new-made peer Lord Saxmundham. He agrees to match Bodger's gift with five thousand pounds of his own, offering it to Mrs Baines in a tone that is 'sardonically gallant'. He points out, with an irony which is lost on Mrs Baines but all too apparent to Barbara, how unselfish he and Bodger are in furthering the Christian mission which is against their own best business interests: 'It is your work to preach peace on earth and goodwill to men. . . . Every convert you make is a vote against war. . . . Yet I give you this money to help you to hasten my own commercial ruin' (CP, III, 133–4). Undershaft is pitiless in showing the sources of the money which is necessary to support the Salvation Army. He fully vindicates his cynical assertion to Cusins: 'All religious organizations exist by selling themselves to the rich' (CP, III, 121).

This revelation is made all the more cruel for Barbara by the desertion of Cusins. Though in the central discussion between the two of them earlier in the act Cusins had resisted Undershaft's arguments, he here joins the millionaire in a conspiracy of irony.

Cusins was hardly a completely convinced member of the Salvation Army at any time. In so far as he had any motive for joining other than love of Barbara it was as a 'collector of religions'. The religion of the Salvation Army means no more, if perhaps no less, to him than the religion of Dionysos. Cusins, with his passion for Euripides, has Euripides' peculiar mixture of ironic rationalism and poetic mysticism. He can let himself go in bursts of dithyrambic enthusiasm while never quite losing a mocking sense of the absurd. It is in 'an ecstasy of mischief', 'a convulsion of irony' that he rushes about the stage organising the triumphant march to the great Salvation Army meeting. There is a terrible pathos in Barbara's appeal to him – 'Dolly: you are breaking my heart' – but he is beyond appeals: 'What is a broken heart more or less here? Dionysos Undershaft has descended. I am possessed' (CP, III, 135).

At the end of the first act the joyful and enthusiastic spirit of the Army, represented by 'Onward Christian Soldiers' on the concertina, won out over the stuffy conventionality of family prayers. At the climax of the second act Barbara's traumatic disillusion and betrayal takes place to the strains of the West Ham Salvation March (actually a 'converted' wedding chorus from Donizetti). She is forced to watch what suddenly seems a grotesque parody of everything that had most attracted her in the Army. Her isolation is enforced by the presence of her father and her lover mockingly joining in the march. The dramatic power of the scene derives from the way in which we are caught between intense sympathy for Barbara and the infectious spirit of drum and tambourine. We are made to participate not only in Barbara's anguish, but in the element of deliberate cruelty in Undershaft and Cusins. Shaw was surely right to defend himself against the charge of blasphemy or irreverence in his use of Christ's cry from the cross:

> *Mrs Baines*: . . . Now Jenny: step out with the old flag. Blood and Fire! [*She marches out through the gate with her flag*].
> *Jenny*: Glory Hallelujah! [*flourishing her tambourine and marching*].
> *Undershaft* [*to Cusins, as he marches out past him easing the slide of his trombone*] : 'My ducats and my daughter'!
> *Cusins* [*following him out*] : Money and gunpowder!
> *Barbara*: Drunkenness and Murder! My God: why hast thou forsaken me? (CP, III, 136)

After this high-point, the final act of the play came for many of the first audiences as a bewildering anti-climax. This was the reaction of Sir Oliver Lodge: 'That second act is great, one of the finest pieces of dramatic art that has been seen for a long time. It is the making of the play, and it leaves one screwed up and tense with feeling. The third act flattens it all out again, and is diabolically cynical.[2] 'Even my cleverest friends', Shaw reported with a touch of pride, 'confessed that the last act beat them; that their brains simply gave way under it' (CL, II, 588). But perhaps it was not only the novelty of the third act or the unfamiliarity of its long and taxing discussion which worried the audiences at the first production; there have been audiences, critics and readers since who have found it less than satisfactory. Shaw himself had great trouble with it. Having completed the play in the summer of 1905, he was forced to re-write the final Act III scene 2 completely in October, just before it went into rehearsal – something he claimed he had never had to do with a play before.[3] What is wrong with the last act of *Major Barbara*? Is it the 'diabolical cynicism' to which Sir Oliver Lodge objected which makes us uneasy, or are there weaknesses in its design and execution?

The theatrical impact of the shift in scene to the munitions works, after the brief return to Wilton Crescent in Act III scene 1, is likely to be effective enough with most audiences. The set horrifyingly illustrates the play's central irony. In the distance we have a view of the Garden City of Perivale St Andrews – 'an almost smokeless town of white walls, roofs of narrow green slates or red tiles, tall trees, campaniles, and slender chimney shafts, beautifully situated and beautiful in itself' (CP, III, 157). After the contrast between urban wealth and urban poverty in the first two acts, we have the futuristic perfection of the modern industrial town. But in the foreground are grim reminders of the way Perivale St Andrews achieves its perfection, the cannon, the high explosives shed, the dummy soldiers. The latter supply a particularly ghastly touch: 'Several dummy soldiers more or less mutilated, with straw protruding from their gashes, have been shoved out of the way under the landing. A few others are nearly upright against the shed; and one has fallen forward and lies, like a grotesque corpse, on the emplacement' (CP, III, 157–8). The effect is of a powerful and near surreal image which with its violent juxtapositions provides a frightening echo of the dramatic action. And yet part of the trouble with this scene is that neither Shaw nor his characters seem to be frightened enough. The talk which ends in the dialectical synthesis of a triple alliance between Cusins, Barbara and Undershaft seems complacent and unreal, untroubled by the implied horrors of the surrounding scene. As Peter Ure puts it acutely, 'Shaw delighted with the characterological neatness of his solution, has not himself troubled to apprehend what really lies behind it'.[4]

The devil's advocacy of Undershaft is the natural development of a technique used from the beginning of Shaw's playwriting career. First Sartorius and then Mrs Warren were used as his spokesmen to shock the audience into realising the truth about their society. The slum-landlord and the brothel-keeper were shown to be necessary products and agents of the capitalist system rather than its unspeakable arch-villains. In *Major Barbara*, which Shaw said might have been more aptly called *Andrew Undershaft's Profession*, it is the turn of the munitions-maker. The function of Undershaft is to challenge the idea of England as a Christian society, devoted to the furtherance of peace, fellowship and goodwill. He points out forcibly that, like any political organisation, it exists by its willingness to use force.

> Let six hundred and seventy fools loose in the streets; and three policemen can scatter them. But huddle them together in a certain house in Westminster; and let them go through certain ceremonies and call themselves certain names until at last they get the courage to kill; and your six hundred and seventy fools become a government. (CP, III, 174)

He reveals that its charitable institutions depend financially on him and his like who make money out of making the instruments of destruction. He believes that there are only two things necessary for salvation: money and gunpower. As Cusins remarks, 'That is the general opinion of our governing classes. The novelty is hearing any man confess it' (CP, III, 116).

The most spectacular tenet of Undershaft's iconoclastic creed is the assertion that poverty is a crime.

> What you call crime is nothing: a murder here and a theft there, a blow now and a curse then: what do they matter? they are only the accidents and illnesses of life: there are not fifty genuine professional criminals in London. But there are millions of poor people, abject people, dirty people, ill fed, ill clothed people. They poison us morally and physically: they kill the happiness of society: they force us to do away with our own liberties and to

organize unnatural cruelties for fear they should rise against us and drag us down into their abyss. (CP, III, 172)

Here, as elsewhere in his work, Shaw is at war with the sentimentalisation of the 'deserving poor' by which society in fact succeeded in evading the real problems of poverty. In the Preface he reinforces Undershaft's viewpoint with a Swiftian modest proposal:

Suppose we were to . . . decide that poverty is the one thing we will not tolerate – that every adult with less than, say, £365 a year, shall be painlessly but inexorably killed, and every hungry half naked child forcibly fattened and clothed, would not that be an enormous improvement on our existing system, which has already destroyed so many civilizations, and is visibly destroying ours in the same way? (CP, III, 26)

This is indeed close to Swift, yet when looked at closely the differences are illuminating. Shaw has not Swift's savage dead-pan irony: his children are to be forcibly fattened for benevolent purposes and the unnecessary adults are to be *painlessly* killed. At various points in his work Shaw made it clear that he thought respect for the sanctity of human life itself greatly exaggerated, but he always tried to dissociate the idea of killing from the deliberate infliction of pain. In the Preface to *On the Rocks* (written in 1933) he says blandly, 'extermination must be put on a scientific basis if it is ever to be carried out humanely and apologetically as well as thoroughly' (CP, VI, 574). In *Caesar and Cleopatra* Caesar praises Rufio for having cut Ftatateeta's throat 'without malice'.

There is a significant ambiguity here which affects the whole technique of devil's advocacy in Shaw. Shaw shrinks from using the fierce tactics of Swift; he pulls his punch in proposing mass executions by adding qualifying phrases about humane-killing. The result is at once to lessen the outrageous impact of the proposal and to give it a partial plausibility. What starts as a shock-tactic, a deliberately horrific suggestion to awaken people's consciences, is palliated to the point where it begins to sound as if it is in earnest. So with Undershaft. As the successor to Sartorius and Mrs Warren, Undershaft's defence of his wicked trade was intended to make us aware of our complicity, our common culpability. But in making Undershaft a model employer and, in spite of his long separation from his wife and family, a near model husband and father, Shaw leaves it hard for us to see that there is much that is diabolic about his devil's advocate. As Desmond MacCarthy said impatiently:

> He talks very big about having been prepared to kill anybody as long as he was poor; but what did he *do*? Did he found his fortunes by knocking an old woman on the head and stealing her watch, or by going into partnership with a Mrs Warren? No, of course not; he stuck to his desk like a good young man, inched and pinched until he had made himself useful to the firm, and then took good care not to be put upon.[5]

Shaw's admiration for Undershaft, his unwillingness to give him any really unpleasant not to mention diabolic traits, produces an imbalance in the play – particularly in the final act. When Gilbert Murray, after hearing the first draft read aloud, complained of the complete victory of Undershaft, Shaw replied, 'that is inevitable because I am in the mind that Undershaft is in the right, and that Barbara and Adolphus, with a great deal of his natural insight and cleverness, are very young, very romantic, very academic, very ignorant of the world' (CL, II, 566). Because of Undershaft's masterfulness, his charm, his eloquence, it seems that we are forced to accept his doctrines at something like face value. Take, for instance, his account of his own success-story:

> *I* was an east ender. I moralized and starved until one day I swore that I would be a full-fed free man at all costs; that nothing should stop me except a bullet, neither reason nor morals nor the lives of other men. I said 'Thou shalt starve ere I starve'; and with that word I became free and great. I was a dangerous man until I had my will: now I am a useful, beneficent, kindly person. That is the history of most self-made millionaires, I fancy. When it is the history of every Englishman we shall have an England worth living in. (CP, III, 173)

This is the naked capitalist ethic of self-help. Does Shaw really believe or want us to believe that a Utopian England is to be achieved by a whole nation of would-be millionaires prepared to cut one another's throats? It seems unlikely, just as it seems improbable that he had abandoned all his Fabian principles of gradualism to endorse Undershaft's thesis that violence is 'the final test of conviction, the only lever strong enough to overturn a social system, the only way of saying Must' (CP, III, 174). And yet within the debating-structure which the play sets up, Undershaft and Undershaftian principles carry the day.

The synthesis represented by the coming together of Barbara, Cusins and Undershaft is suspect partly because Undershaft is too dominant. But there are other difficulties, such as the characterisation of Cusins. Shaw's original plan for the play involved a rather different fiancé for Barbara: in the dramatis personae of the manuscript draft he is cited as 'Dolly Tankerville, 24, heir to a barony, about town at present'.[6] The idea appears to have been to make him a Tweedledum/Tweedledee twin of Cholly Lomax, Sarah's young man. But from the time he began actually writing *Major Barbara*, Shaw changed him to Adolphus Cusins and made him the third most important character. Modelled as he was directly and in detail (down to his Australian birth) on Gilbert Murray the great classicist, Cusins was imagined from the first with a very specific individuality. The introductory character description of him at his first entrance was already there in the manuscript:

His sense of humor is intellectual and subtle, and is complicated by an appalling temper. The lifelong struggle of a benevolent temperament and a high conscience against impulses of inhuman ridicule and fierce impatience has set up a chronic strain which has visibly wrecked his constitution. He is a most implacable, determined, tenacious, intolerant person who by mere force of character presents himself as – and indeed actually is – considerate, gentle, explanatory, even mild and apologetic, capable possibly of murder, but not of cruelty or coarseness. (CP, III, 79–80)

The creation of Cusins was a weird business, with Shaw consulting Murray throughout, quoting his translation of the *Bacchae*, getting help from him with the dialogue, effecting an amazingly direct transposition from life to stage. Murray's comment, as reported by Shaw, is significant: 'He says it is extraordinary how very personal I can be without his seeming to mind, somehow' (CL, II, 591).

Cusins is a firmly realised character. He is perhaps a little too inclined to flaunt his professional interests, and it is now difficult to share Shaw's evident admiration for the Murray translations of Greek tragedy, but he plays a crucial part in the first two acts as both ironic observer and committed participant. The long colloquy between him and Undershaft in the Salvation Army shelter is of great importance in the development of the play's ideas. The two of them flank Barbara symmetrically, as they both, in their different ways, are her suitors. But turning the translator of Euripides into the heir to the Undershaft munitions empire is not so easily managed, for all Undershaft's witty paraphrase of Plato: 'society cannot be saved until either the Professors of Greek take to making gunpowder, or else the makers of gunpowder become Professors of Greek' (CP, III, 178). The plot necessity, the ideological necessity of converting Cusins from Greek teaching to arms making bears heavily on the character, and all the more heavily for the particularity with which the character was conceived. Cusins's arguments against Undershaft in the last act are notably feeble, not only, as Shaw made clear in the passage I have already quoted, because he was 'in the mind that Undershaft was in the right', but because Cusins has been partly reduced to a plot-cipher. The absurdity of his fulfilment of the foundling requirement, the brisk farce of his bargaining for his salary both contribute to the sense of unreality.

Barbara's part in the triple alliance is hardly more fully satisfying than that of Cusins. Once again with Barbara, as with Vivie Warren, Shaw refuses to let his protagonist take her tragedy tragically. When she likens her disillusioning experience at the West Ham shelter to a moral earthquake, her father is contemptuous.

> Come, come, my daughter! dont make too much of your little tinpot tragedy. What do we do here when we spend years of work and thought and thousands of pounds of solid cash on a new gun or an aerial battleship that turns out just a hairsbreadth wrong after all? Scrap it. Scrap it without wasting another hour or another pound on it. Well, you have made for yourself something that you call a morality or a religion or what not. It doesnt fit the facts. Well, scrap it. Scrap it and get one that does fit. That is what is wrong with the world at present. It scraps its obsolete steam engines and dynamos; but it wont scrap its old prejudices and its old moralities and its old religions and its old political constitutions. (CP, III, 170–1)

This, one of the most famous speeches in the play, is some sort of descendant of Mrs Alving's ghosts speech:

> we are all ghosts . . . every one of us. It's not just what we inherit from our mothers and fathers that haunts us. It's all kinds of old

defunct theories, all sorts of old defunct beliefs, and things like that. It's not that they actually *live* on in us; they are simply lodged there, and we cannot get rid of them.[7]

However the contrast is obvious. Ibsen's metaphor which dominates the play is of the inescapable ghosts, the terrible time-lag of understanding behind experience which is beyond human power to change. For Undershaft religious, moral or political theories are merely elaborate hypotheses which could and should be junked as readily as the 'obsolete steam engines and dynamos'. Shaw's whole concept of Creative Evolution is of a divine engineer working forward on a process of trial and error, scrapping remorselessly the unsuccessful models. It is possible to object to the mechanical shallowness of this vision of the world, but that is not the point here. Shaw/Undershaft's breezy rhetoric is invigorating enough, but does it plausibly convince Barbara?

It is absolutely essential to the play's purpose that Barbara should 'return to the colours'. Shaw rejects emphatically the pessimism of disillusionment, as he does the illusionary optimism of the Salvation Army. Barbara's mission must be saved, saved for the real world where it is needed; hence her moral – 'turning our backs on Bodger and Undershaft is turning our backs on life' (CP, III, 183). However, we may assent to this without feeling that Shaw has really shown us how Barbara arrives there emotionally. After all, her metaphor of the earthquake seems justified for what we have seen happen to her in the second act. Surely a character does not move from the despair of 'My God: why hast thou forsaken me?' to the rather knowing moralism of her return to the colours with quite such speed and so little trauma. But emotional and moral trauma Shaw refuses to recognise; for him it is attitudinising, self-indulgence. The characters he admires are not permitted to brood on defeat, they must pick themselves up off the floor and turn defeat into victory. So after the second act which ends with the flatness of Barbara's misery we have the ecstasy which ends the third: 'She has gone right up into the skies.' This is exaltation which seems willed on Shaw's part rather than achieved by Barbara.

It is hard to see just what Barbara and Cusins's marriage and their joint commitment to the Undershaft business means practically. Barbara declares that she will return to the work of salvation, not now among 'weak souls in starved bodies, sobbing with gratitude for a scrap of bread and treacle, but fulfilled, quarrelsome, snobbish, uppish creatures, all standing on their little rights and dignities' (CP,

III, 183). But what exactly will Barbara do with such creatures, the great majority of whom are already Church-going Christians of several different persuasions, and hardly stand in need of conversion? One can only imagine that she will manage and preside in innumerable local committees and take the same sort of benevolent interest in the lives of the workers that her father does. It is a far cry from the mission of the Salvation Army, for all her declaration that 'Major Barbara will die with the colors' (CP, III, 184).

The future of Cusins is even more unclear. He thinks he is joining the munitions industry to sabotage the system from the inside, to 'make war on war'. He renounces the teaching of Greek for its élitism:

> As a teacher of Greek I gave the intellectual man weapons against the common man. I now want to give the common man weapons against the intellectual man. I love the common people. I want to arm them against the lawyers, the doctors, the priests, the literary men, the professors, the artists, and the politicians, who, once in authority, are more disastrous and tyrannical than all the fools, rascals and imposters. I want a power simple enough for common men to use, yet strong enough to force the intellectual oligarchy to use its genius for the general good. (CP, III, 181)

Yet the manufacture of torpedoes and aerial battleships is hardly likely to benefit the common people, or provide the means for them to bring the intellectual oligarchy into their service. Even if red revolution is what Cusins has in mind, how in fact will that be achieved? It is his intention to sell guns to those of whom he approves, to deny them to those he dislikes, but Undershaft insists that he will keep the 'true faith of an Armorer' – 'to give arms to all men who offer an honest price for them, without respect of persons and principles' (CP, III, 168). Here, as throughout this last scene, it is Undershaft with the full weight of his authority and experience who is convincing. At the beginning of the bargaining Cusins warns Undershaft, 'there is an abyss of moral horror between me and your accursed aerial battleships' (CP, III, 165). In the event he does not actually look down into this abyss; he simply shuts his eyes and jumps.

Shaw intended to show in the alliance of Undershaft, Cusins and Barbara a union of power, intellect and moral purpose which was for him the necessary combination for the reformation and salvation of society. 'I am a millionaire;' says Undershaft to Cusins, 'you are a poet; Barbara is a savior of souls. What have we three to do with the common mob of slaves and idolaters?' (CP, III, 120–1). The thrust of *Major Barbara* is to convince us that we need the millionaire, the poet and the saviour of souls, standing above the 'common mob', to make real progress possible. Unfortunately the twentieth century was to provide an all too sinister illustration of what Shaw's supposed ideal looked like in practice. It has been plausibly suggested that the firm of Undershaft and Lazarus was based on Krupps, the German armaments company, the Krupps of the turn of the century having been a notable model employer.[8] Thirty years on, Krupps was to be a crucial if belated supporter of the Nazi party whose programme of rearmament was naturally in the arms industry's best interests. The whole National Socialist movement in fact shows something like the alliance of forces which Shaw asks us to approve in *Major Barbara*. Undershaft's contempt for democracy, for the 'six hundred and seventy fools' calling themselves a government, was of course basic to Nazism. And yet for some of the founding fathers at least it was genuinely socialist and there were notably socialist measures in the early manifestos of the party. There were radical intellectuals in the movement who, like Cusins, believed that they were working for the common people; Goebbels, for example, thought the communists natural allies rather than enemies of the Nazis in the 1920s. Major Barbara's Salvationist enthusiasm, her militant sense of mission was to be reflected on a hugely amplified scale in the Nazi rallies and marches. Hitler and the Nazis were thought by many who supported them to be the saviours of Germany.

This is not to accuse Shaw of proto-Fascism in *Major Barbara*. As Eric Bentley put it, 'his championship of the rightist against the liberal is the old-fashioned devil's advocacy of a Victorian debater rather than the real diabolism that is so common to-day [written in 1947]'.[9] This is well observed; but I do not think Bentley realises how damaging a defence of Shaw it in fact is. It amounts to saying that he does not see the real political implications of his own arguments. Shaw's position in *Major Barbara* is one of innocent totalitarianism. His impatience with the ineptitude and ineffectiveness of conventional political and moral idealism drives him to a eulogy of money and gunpowder. As early as *Cashel Byron's Profession* Shaw has envisioned a union of culture, wealth and 'executive force', and in *Major Barbara* the emphasis falls heavily on the last of the three. This has led one critic to see Shaw in *Major Barbara* as the intellectual heir of Machiavelli, Hobbes and Marx, the theorists of *Realpolitik*.[10] But Shaw's analysis is, when considered closely, a very un-*Realpolitik*. His portrait of Undershaft is of a naturally good man whose natural goodness is expressed in the exercise of power. Shaw believed whole-heartedly in the idea of the benevolent despot, of the great man whose personal will is identical with the best interests of those he governs. If only such great and good men could be given secure control of society, all would be well. Shaw would have emphatically denied Lord Acton's aphorism: 'power tends to corrupt and absolute power corrupts absolutely'; for him those who really deserved power, the Caesars and the Undershafts, were incorruptible. This is, to say the least, a hopeful view of things, and certainly a long way from the spirit of *The Prince* or *Leviathan*.

Major Barbara is a deeply disquieting play, but not in the way Shaw intended it to be. Shaw's initial aim was to bring home what was to become a major Brechtian message – 'bread before morals'. Undershaft argues cogently that it was his money that 'saved' Barbara: 'I fed you and clothed you and housed you. I took care that you should have money enough to live handsomely – more than enough; so that you could be wasteful, careless, generous' (CP, III, 171). Unless people's bodies are well cared for, there is no point in concerning oneself with their souls. And therefore it is the producers of wealth in the society, however unpalatable the way that the wealth is produced, who make possible any sort of moral or religious mission. Without material power, Shaw argues in *Major Barbara*, spiritual power is meaningless. Hence the final test of conviction is the willingness to kill for what one believes. If we are prepared to face that and use the power to kill for good rather than evil, then we may begin to make progress. There is, however, a devastating force in Undershaft's disillusionment of Barbara and a horror in the image of the clean and well – organised arms factory which makes it hard for us to accept what Shaw wanted to be the optimism of the ending. It is not that we shrink from the hard truths which the play expresses – the reaction Shaw was inclined to attribute to audiences of his works. What is disturbing is rather his wilful refusal to follow through the implications of these hard truths himself, his tendency to soften them into the complacent attitudes of the debating chamber. In his celebration of will and power in Undershaft, in his conversion of Barbara's zeal and Cusins's mind to the service of will and power, Shaw does not seem to see that he has given the devil much more than his due.

7 The Perfection of Levity

In 1897, when Shaw was planning *Caesar and Cleopatra* for Johnston Forbes Robertson and Mrs Patrick Campbell, he wrote to Ellen Terry that he had been temporarily distracted: 'Caesar and Cleopatra has been driven clean out of my head by a play I want to write for them in which he shall be a west end gentleman and she an east end dona in an apron and three orange and red ostrich feathers.'[1] It was fifteen years before he wrote a line of *Pygmalion*, but when finally written it was still a vehicle for Mrs Patrick Campbell (though she had changed her leading man from Forbes Robertson to Beerbohm Tree) and the hat with three ostrich feathers remained a feature. Once again it is remarkable how clear and how unchanged Shaw could carry the idea of a play for years before execution. But the prevision of *Pygmalion* glimpsed in the letter to Ellen Terry serves also to highlight the play's formal relation to the earlier period of his career. In 1897 he was still working within the popular forms of the time, writing melodrama and romance to challenge the audiences' melodramatic and romantic expectations. In many ways *Pygmalion* is a Pleasant Play, a Play for Puritans, written out of its time. In the major trilogy of 1901–5, *Man and Superman*, *John Bull's Other Island* and *Major Barbara*, Shaw had developed his own discursive form of comedy of ideas. In the plays that followed he defied audience expectations of formal structure even more recklessly; *Getting Married* (1908) and *Misalliance* (1909) are almost pure discussion plays and Shaw was proud of their plotlessness. 'Surely nobody expects a play by me to have a plot. I am a dramatic poet not a plotmonger' (CP, III, 667). In *Pygmalion*, by contrast, Shaw returned to his earlier technique of giving his audience what appeared to be the popular romance they wanted but with anti-romantic Shavian treatment. As everyone knows, the popular romance was gobbled up and the ironic reinterpretation ignored.

However, it was not only because *Pygmalion's* immense success was achieved at the expense of his artistic intentions that Shaw was to dismiss the play contemptuously as a potboiler. He never could stand the popularity of his own most popular works. His dislike for *Arms and the Man*, *The Devil's Disciple* or *Candida* grew in proportion to the enthusiasm of their admirers. Many writers get tired of being praised for their successful works and are protective towards their less loved creations, so there is nothing out of the way in Shaw's preference for that most elephantine of ugly ducklings, *Back to Methusaleh*, over his most graceful swans. But the 'potboiler' *Pygmalion* raises very real critical and evaluative problems. It is a more limited, a less ambitious play than, say, *Major Barbara*; yet it has a dazzling perfection of form and execution which Shaw never achieved in his full-scale 'major' works, a perfection of form neither trivial nor empty. Peter Ure is hardly overstating the case when he says 'It is simply one of the very greatest of English comedies'.[2] If we are to come to terms with the nature of Shaw's dramatic achievement we must account for a play which is one of his most assured successes yet seemed to him in some sort a mere five-finger exercise.

> I wish to boast that Pygmalion has been an extremely successful play, both on stage and screen,[3] all over Europe and North America as well as at home. It is so intensely and deliberately didactic, and its subject is esteemed so dry, that I delight in throwing it at the heads of the wiseacres who repeat the parrot cry that art should never be didactic. It goes to prove my contention that great art can never be anything else. (CP, IV, 663)

This quotation, and the whole Preface to *Pygmalion* from which it is taken, seem to represent Shaw at his most perverse, pretending that the play is a tract about phonetics rather than a Cinderella romance. And yet *Pygmalion* does express Shavian teaching on certain issues as acutely as his more obviously didactic works. The play may not be about phonetics as such, but its focus on speech and accent make possible a radical critique of a class-based society, all the more piquant for its indirectness. In dramatising the metamorphosis of flower-girl into lady, Shaw not only feeds our fairy-tale fantasies; he challenges the assumption that there is anything more to gentility than money and the arbitrary shibboleths of social behaviour. Socially we are what we sound like, and if we can change our voices we change ourselves.

In *Pygmalion* Shaw explores the interrelations of language, class and money. What Eliza wants from Higgins is a specific step upward in the world:

I want to be a lady in a flower shop stead of sellin at the corner of Tottenham Court Road. But they wont take me unless I can talk more genteel. He said he could teach me. Well here I am ready to pay him. (CP, IV, 688)

On a grander scale this is indeed Higgins's business:

This is an age of upstarts. Men begin in Kentish Town with £80 a year, and end in Park Lane with a hundred thousand. They want to drop Kentish Town; but they give themselves away every time they open their mouths. Now I can teach them. (CP, IV, 679)

But it is not only for the upstarts, the ex-Kentish Towners, that language as class-index is important; it is just as crucial for Shaw's own class of 'downstarts', the Eynsford Hills of Earl's Court (Bayswater in an earlier version). The wonderful comedy of Act III derives from the way in which Eliza's 'small talk' is misconstrued. The Eynsford Hills, conscious always of their limited means to sustain their upper-class manners, take Eliza's all too natural profanities for the latest chic. It is because both she and they are *déclassés* that the comedy of misunderstanding can continue to its climax in the notorious 'Not bloody likely!'

There is more than mere comical absurdity in Eliza's pure diction and social solecisms in this scene. What we see in Mrs Higgins's At Home is a real clash of cultures. While we laugh at the wild indecorum of Eliza's conversation, we register the enormous gulf between the world she comes from and the world of the Eynsford Hills. We may not take quite literally the picture of Eliza's aunt miraculously cured of diphtheria by unlimited quantities of gin ladled down her throat, nor yet the dark suspicion that she was finally murdered:

What call would a woman with that strength in her have to die of influenza? What become of her new straw hat that should have come to me? Somebody pinched it; and what I say is, them as pinched it done her in. (CP, IV, 729)

But the effect is to make vivid for us Eliza's background in which possessions were sufficiently few to make the inheritance of a hat a matter of moment. When Mrs Eynsford Hill is horrified at Eliza's revelation that her father 'drank', she is reassured:

It never did him no harm what I could see. But then he did not keep it up regular. [*Cheerfully*] On the burst, as you might say, from time to time. And always more agreeable when he had a drop in. When he was out of work, my mother used to give him fourpence and tell him to go out and not come back until he'd drunk himself cheerful and loving-like. (CP, IV, 729–30)

For all its comic context, it is hard to imagine a more caustic comment on the traditional pieties of drink as the curse of the working classes.

Lightly, yet pervasively throughout the play, Shaw reminds us of the miseries of poverty, the all-importance of money for decent human life. Higgins, for example, has a mannerism of walking up and down jingling the coins in his pocket. It is one of the small details which serve to bring the character alive before us in all his individuality. Yet it suggests with great tact that some measure of Higgins's bullying self-confidence derives from the unquestioned security of ample means. This is the more striking for the gesture at the end of Act I where the handful of this rattling loose change which Higgins throws to Eliza is seen to represent a small fortune to her. Social commentary in *Pygmalion* is made not tendentiously but casually, obliquely. When Mrs Pearce suggests that Eliza may be married, Higgins dismisses the idea with scorn: 'Dont you know that a woman of that class looks a worn out drudge of fifty a year after she's married?' (CP, IV, 693). Eliza returns from her bath, amazed at the delights of the bathroom: 'Now I know why ladies is so clean. Washing's a treat for them' (CP, IV, 714). The ordinary amenities which Shaw's Edwardian audience would have taken for granted are unheard of luxuries for the likes of Eliza. And among such amenities are the niceties of moral feeling. 'Have you no morals, man?' the outraged Pickering demands of Doolittle.

> Doolittle [*unabashed*]: Cant afford them, Governor. Neither could you if you was as poor as me. (CP, IV, 710)

Doolittle is, of course, one of the main spokesmen for Shaw's social satire:

What am I, Governors both? I ask you, what am I? I'm one of the undeserving poor: thats what I am. Think of what that means to a man. It means that he's up agen middle class morality all the time. If theres anything going, and I put in for a bit of it, it's always the same story: 'Youre undeserving; so you cant have it.' But my needs is as great as the most deserving widow's that ever got money out of six different charities in one week for the death of the same husband. I dont need less than a deserving man: I need more. I dont eat less hearty than him; and I drink a lot more. I want a bit of amusement, cause I'm a thinking man. I want cheerfulness and a song and a band when I feel low. Well, they charge me just the same for everything as they charge the deserving. What is middle class morality? Just an excuse for never giving me anything. (CP, IV, 711)

This is a splendid send-up of the whole concept of the 'deserving poor' so dear to Victorian philanthropy. Within a society still dominated by the principles of economic individualism, the poor were not entitled to support as of right but had to prove that they morally deserved charity. But it is not only the hypocritical rhetoric of 'middle-class morality' which Shaw mocks through Doolittle, it is the basic principle of the bourgeois society. When Higgins finally decides to give Doolittle a fiver, Pickering – so often used as straight man in the play – comments with conventional disapproval, 'He'll make a bad use of it, I'm afraid.' Doolittle picks this up and turns it on its head:

Not me, Governor, so help me I wont. Dont you be afraid that I'll save it and spare it and live idle on it. There wont be a penny of it left by Monday: I'll have to go to work same as if I'd never had it. It wont pauperise me, you bet. Just one good spree for myself and the missus, giving pleasure to ourselves and employment to others, and satisfaction to you to think it's not been throwed away. You couldnt spend it better. (CP, IV, 712)

Prudent saving, from the bourgeois point of view, is virtue; reckless spending is vice. But the object of saving is the accumulation of capital which will make it possible to live without working in the future. And thus in Shaw/Doolittle's mock logic, thrift is motivated by the desire for idleness. One of the commonest objections to general and systematic support for the poor in Victorian England was that it would 'pauperise' them, that is accustom them to living off hand-outs like paupers. (We still hear the same argument from those who inveigh against 'social security scroungers'.) But, Shaw

implies, those who save to live off unearned income are just as
effectively pauperised. We are close here to the heart of Shaw's
opposition to capitalism. It was not merely the inequitable distribution of wealth within the capitalist society to which he objected,
but the inequitable distribution of work. A work-ethic was fundamental to Shaw's temperament and he could never accept a system
in which a proportion of people were permitted to do nothing.

The purpose of Doolittle's visit to Wimpole Street is to sell his
daughter:

> Regarded in the light of a young woman, she's a fine handsome
> girl. As a daughter she's not worth her keep; and so I tell you
> straight. All I ask is my rights as a father; and youre the last man
> alive to expect me to let her go for nothing; for I can see youre one
> of the straight sort, Governor. Well, whats a five-pound note to
> you? and whats Eliza to me? (CP, IV, 710)

As far back as *Mrs Warren's Profession* Shaw had insisted on the
inherent meretriciousness of the capitalist society, and he was to
make the same point again forcefully later:

> Capitalism acts on women as a continual bribe to enter into sex
> relations for money, whether in or out of marriage; and against
> this bribe there stands nothing beyond the traditional respectabil-
> ity which Capitalism ruthlessly destroys by poverty, except
> religion and the inborn sense of honor which has its citadel in the
> soul and can hold out (sometimes) against all circumstances.[4]

Eliza has such an 'inborn sense of honor', however comically voiced
in her recurrent cries of 'I'm a good girl, I am'. She reacts with bitter
pride in Act IV when Higgins suggests that the problem of her future
would be solved by marrying:

> *Higgins*: . . . I daresay my mother could find some chap or other
> who would do very well.
> *Liza*: We were above that at the corner of Tottenham Court
> Road.
> *Higgins* [*waking up*]: What do you mean?
> *Liza*: I sold flowers. I didnt sell myself. Now youve made a lady of
> me I'm not fit to sell anything else. (CP, IV, 750)

Eliza is treated as a property by Higgins and Pickering. They may not want her for the purposes which Doolittle thinks they do, but she is a property to them none the less. They are fascinated by the game of transforming her into a lady and refuse to consider the human implications of that game. Although Pickering is superficially more polite and considerate to Eliza, he like Higgins is fundamentally unaware of her as a person, as we can see from their joint chorus to Mrs Higgins in Act III and their common insensitivity to Eliza's feelings in Act IV. Mrs Higgins speaks for Shaw's feminism as Doolittle for his socialism. 'You certainly are a pretty pair of babies, playing with your live doll' (CP, IV, 734). Shaw equates the egotism of the sexist male with the egotism of the child who cannot recognise the autonomous existence of others.

It is possible thus to make good Shaw's claim that *Pygmalion* is a didactic play. Though the teaching on class, money and social attitudes may be expressed with the light-heartedness of a comedy of manners, it is pointedly there all the same. But the play is not a Shavian tract with comic overlay. If it were, it is likely that by now it would seem extremely dated instead of being one of the most perennially popular of Shaw's works. Speech and accent are no longer the audible expression of class, or at least not in the simple sense that they were for *Pygmalion*'s first audiences. A received standard upper-class voice, such as Higgins teaches Eliza to have, may now be as much a social liability as an asset. Much of the play's social analysis scarcely seems applicable to contemporary English (or any other) society. The fate of the shabby-genteel, the Eynsford Hills, brought up to do nothing and given nothing to do it on, seems a peculiarly Edwardian plight. Eliza, educated to speak and behave like a lady, would not any more find herself disqualified from employment as a result. The gap between rich and poor has narrowed at least to the extent that Eliza's modern-day equivalent would not be overwhelmed at a handful of money thrown into her basket, nor awed at the luxuries of the bathroom. Yet *Pygmalion* has not dated, as it would have done if its party political points had been its main *raison d'être*. At this distance in time it stands instead as a great comedy in a period setting.

The comedy, and above all the comic characterisation in *Pygmalion*, depend upon rather different assumptions than the social satire. As a play about metamorphosis, the miraculous change of Eliza from flower-girl to lady, with its comic counterpart in

Doolittle's transformation from dustman to gentleman, it appears to express a socialist conviction that human beings are created and conditioned by the arbitrary contingencies of their society. People are social animals and may become very different animals in different social circumstances. *Pygmalion*, with its thesis that a lady is only a flower-girl plus six months' stiff phonetic training, a gentleman only a dustman with money, would seem to be the ultimate affirmation of that view. But, as many critics have been quick to point out, Eliza is not just any flower-girl and Doolittle is most certainly not a representative dustman. And, what is more important, they are recognisably the same people before and after metamorphosis. Higgins may claim to have created Eliza out of 'squashed cabbage leaves', but the flower-girl of Act I, however bedraggled, must still be seen to be there in the perfect lady who sits in Act V sewing in Mrs Higgins's Chelsea drawing-room. Doolittle is still Doolittle on his second appearance, for all his top hat and St George's Hanover Square outfit.

The main characters in *Pygmalion* have that special integrity which belongs to the comic tradition. Doolittle, one of Shaw's most genial comic creations, is a case in point. His great speech on the undeserving poor, quoted earlier, is an instrument of Shaw's social satire. But Doolittle's sedition of social orthodoxies is more radical and more anarchic than that. His anatomy of middle-class morality is like Falstaff's catechism on honour, a total subversion of normal values. Some critics have evidently been shocked by Doolittle's Falstaffian shamelessness: Louis Crompton comments disapprovingly, 'If we leave his engaging impudence aside, it is a difficult thing to admire a man who wants to sell his daughter, and it is impossible to like a blackmailer.'[5] But we are not permitted to leave his engaging impudence aside; it disarms us into liking, even admiring Doolittle for all his pimping and blackmailing, just as we are disarmed into liking Falstaff. Doolittle and Falstaff speak from a fulness of comic personality which is so purely itself that it leaves no room for ordinary moral judgement. We laugh at them partly out of a delighted enjoyment of their iconoclasm, their unabashed defiance of inhibiting proprieties, but also out of a shared sense of their enjoyment of themselves. In the final act Doolittle may proclaim that he has been 'ruined' by his inheritance, is now intimidated by middle-class morality, but it is hard to believe him. Doolittle, whether dustman or lecturer extraordinary to the Wannafeller Moral Reform World League, is what he is.

The character of Higgins is the glory of *Pygmalion*. Higgins is high comedy, a long way from the fixity of humours characterisation, yet he too is unchanging and unchangeable. Shaw took a realist's care with the minutiae of Higgins's individuality. For example, in the first published versions of the play he was an amateur poet as well as a professor of phonetics; he explained to Pickering that on the profits of his teaching, 'I do genuine scientific work in phonetics, and a little as a poet on Miltonic lines'.[6] Shaw seems to have seen that it was a false note to have Higgins a neo-classical poetaster and cut the reference out of the revised text. Higgins's cult of Milton remains in the phrase 'the treasures of my Miltonic mind', but his poetic calling only survives in his defence of bloodying the boots, the butter and the brown bread – 'Mere alliteration, Mrs Pearce, natural to a poet' (CP, IV, 703). Higgins's austere aesthetic tastes are suggested by the laboratory in Wimpole Street: 'On the walls, engravings: mostly Piranesis and mezzotint portraits. No paintings' (CP, IV, 685). But in amusing contrast to such austerity is his childish sweet tooth, 'the dessert dish heaped with fruit and sweets, mostly chocolates' at which he nibbles or munches habitually. All of such details are there to realise Higgins with a vivid and immediate presence, enabling us to take in the whole of his personality at once. His physical mannerisms contribute to the same effect. We know him by the restless energy which never lets him stay still, by the stage movements he is given: when he is talking to Pickering 'lifting himself on his hands to the level of the piano, and sitting on it with a bounce' (CP, IV, 701), or when he is wrecking his mother's At Home – 'He goes to the divan, stumbling into the fender and over the fire-irons on his way; extricating himself with muttered imprecations; and finishing his disastrous journey by throwing himself so impatiently on the divan that he almost breaks it' (CP, IV, 728). Higgins has that superabundant specificity of life which makes for a great stage comic character.

Higgins is impossible, his treatment of those around him is atrociously insensitive, he is a tyrannical egotist, and yet we delight in his impossibility, his insensitivity, his egotism. We do so by virtue of the special licence offered to the overgrown children of comedy. Shaw's stage direction tells us that Higgins is

but for his years and size, rather like a very impetuous baby 'taking notice' eagerly and loudly, and requiring almost as much watching to keep him out of unintended mischief. His manner varies from genial bullying when he is in a good humor to stormy petulance when anything goes wrong; but he is so entirely frank and void of malice that he remains likeable even in his least reasonable moments. (CP, IV, 685)

The phrase 'frank and void of malice' is a characteristically Shavian term of indulgence, but the whole description gives us the key-note to Higgins's comic infantilism. It is in this also that his dependence on his mother is significant. Higgins at some level has never grown up, as he reveals in a genuinely bewildered and splendidly unselfaware speech to Pickering about Mrs Pearce:

> You know, Pickering, that woman has the most extraordinary ideas about me. Here I am, a shy, diffident sort of man. Ive never been able to feel really grown-up and tremendous, like other chaps. And yet she's firmly persuaded that I'm an arbitrary over-bearing bossing kind of person. I cant account for it. (CP, IV, 705)

In Higgins's explosions of wrath, in his appalling tyranny of manner, we see an adult of exceptional force and articulateness behave with the emotional ruthlessness of a child. We ought to be revolted by his genial contempt for Eliza:

> *Pickering* [*in good-humored remonstrance*]: Does it occur to you, Higgins, that the girl has some feelings?
> *Higgins* [*looking critically at her*]: Oh no, I dont think so. Not any feelings that we need bother about. [*Cheerily*] Have you, Eliza? (CP, IV, 694–5)

But instead we enjoy the sheer outrageousness with which he is allowed to disregard the human decencies, and in our enjoyment is mingled a certain vicarious pleasure in the rampant egotism which in ordinary social life we dare not allow ourselves.

In the clash between Higgins and Eliza, however, ego meets defiant ego. From the first there is that in Eliza which resists Higgins and which makes her finally his match. For all the enormous superiority of class and money which Higgins uses unmercifully in the scene in Covent Garden, Eliza holds on firmly, comically, pathetically to her sense of her rights: 'Aint no call to meddle with me, he aint', 'He's no right to take away my character. My character is the same to me as any lady's, (CP, IV, 676, 678). They are at cross-purposes from the beginning and remain so throughout much of the play. When Higgins resorts to 'the most thrillingly beautiful low tones in his best elocutionary style' to impress Eliza, she is unimpressed: 'I'm going away. He's off his chump, he is. I dont want no balmies teaching me' (CP, IV, 693). Yet the comedy of cross-purposes would not be so funny if it did not involve the feeling that Eliza is ultimately able to stand up to Higgins's bullying. This is not to deny that he can cause her real suffering, that his wanton insensitivity amounts to cruelty at times. But Eliza was never the 'squashed cabbage leaves' that Higgins took her for; this is a special version of the Pygmalion legend in which Galathea is alive from the start.

The relationship between Higgins and Eliza, and particularly its conclusion, has become *the* critical question of *Pygmalion*. From the moment that Beerbohm Tree evaded Shaw's clear directions and contrived to suggest a romantic ending by throwing flowers to Eliza just before the final curtain (on a purely theatrical level a nice touch, reversing the image at the end of Act I where Eliza threw her flowers at Higgins), the argument was on. Shaw was outraged, and wrote his polemic epilogue to show that Eliza actually married Freddy. There appears to be no truth in the supposition that he countenanced the ending of the Gabriel Pascal film which also suggested a Higgins/Eliza union.[7] Certainly in his own original screenplay Shaw insisted in his opening description of Higgins,

> It is important that in age and everything else he should be in strong contrast to Freddy, who is 20, slim, goodlooking, and very youthful.
>
> (The producer should bear in mind from the beginning that it is Freddy who captivates and finally carries off Eliza, and that all suggestion of a love interest between Eliza and Higgins should be most carefully avoided.)[8]

There remains a strong suspicion on the part of many readers and audiences that the refusal to allow Eliza to marry Higgins is a piece of Shavian perversity, a denial of the play's natural ending.[9]

It is possible to admire Shaw's ending as a fitting conclusion to the relationship between Higgins and Eliza, and yet to admit that there is a degree of evasiveness in its treatment. It its rejection of sexual consummation some critics have seen the expression of Shaw's own peculiar psycho-sexual history, both his Oedipal feelings for his mother who died not long after he finished the play, and his

relationship with Mrs Patrick Campbell, the leading lady, with
whom he had the one passionate (if unconsummated) affair of his
long celibate married life.[10] Whatever *Pygmalion*'s psychoanalytic
origins, one speech of Higgins in the final scene with Eliza is very
striking:

> If you cant stand the coldness of my sort of life, and the strain of it,
> go back to the gutter. Work til youre more a brute than a human
> being; and then cuddle and squabble and drink til you fall asleep.
> Oh, it's a fine life, the life of the gutter. It's real: it's warm: it's
> violent: you can feel it through the thickest skin: you can taste it
> and smell it without any training or any work. Not like Science
> and Literature and Classical Music and Philosophy and Art. You
> find me cold, unfeeling, selfish, dont you? Very well: be off with
> you to the sort of people you like. Marry some sentimental hog or
> other with lots of money, and a thick pair of lips to kiss you with
> and a thick pair of boots to kick you with. If you cant appreciate
> what youve got, youd better get what you can appreciate. (CP,
> IV, 779)

There is much here that seems to speak from somewhere deep within
Shaw – the fear of emotion and of sexuality expressed with a violence
that amounts to sadism, and the association of that fear with the
refinements of a high culture. This is Shaw's version of civilisation
and its discontents. Through Higgins he contrives to suggest that the
sexual bond is necessarily sado-masochistic and that the only
alternative, other than the emotional dependence of the relationship
of Higgins to his mother, is the sexless companionship with Eliza of a
continued life with Pickering as 'three old bachelors together'. The
marriage with Freddy, based on what Higgins despises as the
'commercial principles' of mutual need, though Shaw may have
defended its versimilitude in the epilogue, is experienced in the play
as a banal and superficial second-best.

And yet this is not to say that the Higgins/Eliza marriage is
deliberately withheld for extradramatic reasons of Shaw's own. The
final unresolved conflict between the two is the right ending for the
play because it is the ultimate expression of the inalienable
individuality of each. Higgins by temperament and situation has
always bullied and domineered over Eliza; it has always been her
instinct to defend herself and resist that bullying. The irony of the
final situation is that his teaching has given her sufficient skill and

self-confidence to resist him successfully, and this in turn inspires his respect: 'By George, Eliza, I said I'd make a woman of you; and I have. I like you like this' (CP, IV, 781). But Eliza will not settle for less than love and that Higgins will not, cannot give her, because he cannot give himself to another person. Some critics have argued that the scene represents the victory of one over the other, and in that victory an illustration of Shavian principle: for Eric Bentley 'Eliza turns the tables on Higgins' to show vitality emerging from system;[11] for Louis Crompton on the other hand, it is Higgins with his 'passion for improving the race' who is superior to Eliza with her 'ordinary human desire for the comforts and consolations of the domestic hearth'.[12] But surely the ending is intended rather as a deliberately poised comic stasis. It is like the great final scene between Alceste and Célimène in Molière's *Misanthrope* in which *rapprochement* is impossible because, for all their attractions to one another, the characters are so unchangeably themselves. It was often claimed that in the Alceste/Célimène relationship Molière was writing out of his own experience; for whatever reasons Shaw also deeply understands both sides of the Higgins/Eliza confrontation. But in each case what the playwright gives us is the wholeness of a comically perceived situation in which we can enjoy the frustrations of the incompatible pair as fully as ever we do the fulfilments of the lovers in romantic comedy.

Shaw would not have classified *Pygmalion* as one of his major plays and no more do most of his critics. And yet can we possibly call such a sustained and enduring comic masterpiece a minor work? It lacks major status within the Shaw canon because it is without the driving dialectic of plays such as *Man and Superman*, *Major Barbara* or *Saint Joan*. Although *Pygmalion* has plenty to say on favourite Shaw topics, it is not structured towards the expression of his central vision. But for that very reason it seems an especially free gift of his comic creativity. It is hard to do justice to the play in these terms, to avoid making it seem a merely delightful entertainment, a diversion from the more doctrinal Shaw. However, if comedy itself is to be regarded as more than a superficial and trivial genre, then the brilliant conception of the dramatic fable in *Pygmalion*, the fulness and richness of its comic characterisation deserve more than faint praise. So many of Shaw's works on a larger scale remain to some extent flawed and unsatisfying that we cannot afford to undervalue the unique success of *Pygmalion*, even if its very successfulness makes it look easily achieved.

8 Bangs and Whimpers

Heartbreak House, slated by reviewers both when it was published in 1919 and when it was first produced in London in 1921, is now claimed by many Shaw critics to be perhaps his greatest play. It is interesting to speculate on the reasons for this rise in its reputation. Formally, it represents something of a new departure for Shaw, with a technique and structure which can be compared with more modern dramatists. Its use of symbolism, its allusiveness, its free adaptation of the Chekhovian style, relate it to the Modernist mode. It becomes a key talking-point, therefore, in the defence of Shaw against the common complaint that his dramaturgy is old-fashioned and limited. Indeed its atypicality within the Shavian canon wins the play praise from those who are critical of Shaw's other plays: for Robert Brustein in his study of the modern 'theatre of revolt', it is outstanding;[1] even Francis Fergusson, one of Shaw's severest critics, makes a partial exception of *Heartbreak House*.[2] It is not only in technique but in mood and theme that the play appears more akin to the major works of the twentieth century than anything else Shaw wrote. Its intimations of apocalypse seem to relate it to the great literary creations to emerge from the First World War.

The play represents, for more than one critic, a response to the war which deepened and darkened Shaw's drama into a tragic vision.[3] Shaw, so often judged incapable of tragedy, himself cites *Heartbreak House* in his defence, in his nonagenarian mock debate with Shakespeare, *Shakes versus Shav*:

> *Shakes*: Where is thy Hamlet? Couldst thou write King Lear?
> *Shav*: Aye, with his daughters all complete. Couldst thou have written Heartbreak House? Behold my Lear. (CP, VII, 475)

It is, moreover, specifically a tragic vision for and of its time, Shaw having moved on from the spirit of his earlier work. As Alfred Turco puts it, 'if *Major Barbara* had been the culmination of nineteenth-century optimism, *Heartbreak House* is the harbinger of twentieth-century despair'.[4] This seems the more striking because on the whole Shaw's career shows so few signs of change and development. There is a remarkable homogeneity about Shaw's drama; many of his outstanding characteristics as a playwright seem to have been set by the end of the 1890s and to have altered little thereafter. Against this sense of Shavian sameness, it is tempting to see *Heartbreak House* as the discovery of a new tragic maturity born of the anguish of the war.

There are then good reasons why the play's reputation should stand as high as it does. But they are, to some extent, reasons contingent upon the nature of Shaw's reputation generally and the atypical form and mood of *Heartbreak House*. For the play's first reviewers, it was laboured, incoherent and shapeless – 'half-procession, half-pandemonium', Middleton Murry called it[5] – and some later critics have been inclined to agree.[6] It remains debatable whether this is simply an obtuse refusal to respond to the unusual mode of *Heartbreak House* or whether the play may not have real weaknesses of structure, real uncertainties of artistic intention. What I wish to do in this chapter is to examine the achievement of *Heartbreak House* in relation to the high claims made for it, to see how well the post-Chekhovian mode of the play's form and technique suited Shaw, and whether we can really find in it the signs of a new tragic vision in his work.

In sub-titling *Heartbreak House* 'A Fantasia in the Russian Manner on English Themes', in highlighting the influence of Tchekhov (as he was still then transliterated) on him in the Preface, Shaw laid himself open for all future critics to use Chekhov as a stick to beat him with. *Heartbreak House* is unChekhovian in all sorts of obvious ways that were very quickly pointed out. But the contrast between Shaw and Chekhov is still sufficiently instructive to make it a useful starting-point for the discussion of the Shavian version of *The Cherry Orchard*. What seems perhaps most striking is Shaw's difficulty with the dramatic focus on the ensemble which is Chekhov's particular distinction. Chekhov worked always with a group – the extended family centring on the country house or estate, the circle surrounding the three sisters. Within that group there are central figures, of course, but the over-all dramatic composition involves the blending of a number of sharply individualised characters of almost equal importance. Chekhov's plays demand ensemble acting; they cannot be played on the centripetal star system. Shaw's whole dramatic technique, by contrast, is built upon the nineteenth-century tradition of a small number of central characters. In the great majority of

Shaw plays there are one, two or most often three big starring parts which dominate and, though he could write marvellous supporting character roles, they were carefully subordinated within the play's structure.

We can see even within *Heartbreak House* signs of this normal Shaw principle of organisation. Captain Shotover (undoubtedly) and Ellie Dunn (less certainly) are planned as leading parts. But he deliberately adopted the Chekhovian wider focus and the more democratic distribution of weight and interest among the characters, with some awkward results. Through Act I Shaw manages the separate entrances of his eight major characters with great skill. The several visitors, Ellie, Lady Utterword, Mazzini Dunn, Mangan and Randall are all deftly defined in their bewilderment at the house and its occupants. Shaw works to splendid comic effect with the disorienting atmosphere of Heartbreak House represented most signally by the wayward appearances and disappearances of Shotover. The random disjointedness of the action is, throughout the first act, visibly in the control of a comic dramatist giving point and purpose to the cross-purposes and inconsequence. But the effect of the enormously long Act II is very different. Shaw here rings the changes upon his several characters, giving us some seven separate *tête-à-tête* scenes interspersed only occasionally by group interludes in which all or most of the characters are on stage together. Each one of these scenes has a characteristically Shavian clash of characters – the blustering Mangan totally flabbergasted by Ellie's new-found cool cynicism, Mrs Hushabye unexpectedly charmed by the apparently priggish Mazzini Dunn, Ellie facing up to the previously patronising Mrs Hushabye and fighting it out over Hector, and so on. But each encounter seems distinct, autonomous, and it becomes increasingly hard to feel that there is a dramatic continuity to sustain our attention and interest. By the end of the act we are likely to be as bewildered as the most bewildered member of Heartbreak House, dazed by the relentless sequence of unrelated emotional fireworks.

Chekhov's technique was to allow the action apparently to drift inconsequentially along, while the real dramatic pattern is shaped through the indirect suggestiveness of mood, symbol and subtext. In *Heartbreak House* the action never drifts but proceeds forward in a series of galvanic jerks. Towards the end of Act I, for instance, à propos of nothing at all, Mrs Hushabye suddenly calls Shotover and Hector back as they are about to leave the room, to announce that 'Money is running short'. Shotover is told off to sit down to his drawing-board and invent something to provide further income. The incident serves to highlight both the extravagance of Heartbreak House and the role of Shotover as inventor, but otherwise it seems unrelated to anything which comes before or after. Again the incident in Act II when Ellie hypnotises Mangan is disconcerting. Shaw had shown an interest in hypnotism and trance already in *Getting Married*, and Ellie's hypnotic powers no doubt contribute to the sense of her affinity with Shotover, but one cannot help suspecting that the whole episode is largely a device to enable Mangan to overhear the two revealing scenes that follow. The burglar incident, above all, is the most notorious example of Shaw's disregard for the *liaison des scènes* in *Heartbreak House*. A number of critics have defended it for its symbolic value as 'a kernel into which many of the play's distinct themes have been compressed'.[7] By making the burglar turn out to be Billy Dunn, the ex-pirate, Mazzini Dunn's comic alter ego and Nurse Guinness's long-lost husband, Shaw justifies the character according to the laws of farcical comedy, and by linking him in death with Mangan – 'the two burglars – the two practical men of business' – he scores a final thematic point. But the anomalous and arbitrary impression made by the burglar scene remains, all the more so for Shaw's over-ingenious attempt to integrate it into the plot.

A comparison with a minor incident in *The Cherry Orchard* again reinforces the dissimilarity of Chekhov and Shaw's dramatic technique. In Act II, with most of the cast assembled out of doors towards evening, just after the famous sound of the snapping string, a Tramp wanders on to the stage looking for the way to the station. The characters react in a typical variety of ways, Varia is frightened, Lopakhin is indignant, Ranevskaya is thoughtlessly generous in response to the Tramp's begging, but they are all vaguely startled and alarmed. The Tramp with his snatches of poetry serves as a mocking parody of the effusive and declamatory Gaev; as a representative of the homeless and dispossessed he is also, at some level, an ominous figure for the family about to lose their estate. But the suggestiveness of the Tramp is managed entirely within the naturalistic verisimilitude of a stray incident. Shaw cannot manage the sort of looseness of dramatic texture in which such underplayed episodes are unobtrusive. Instead his burglar scene becomes a big set-piece, highlighting its own disconnectedness and Shaw's all too deliberate efforts to connect it.

There is evidence from the history of the play's composition that

Shaw was not at home with the form and style of *Heartbreak House*. The idea for the play had apparently been in his mind for several years before he began to write it in March 1916.[8] In May he wrote a depressed non-progress report to Mrs Patrick Campbell: 'I am old and finished. I who once wrote whole plays *d'un seul trait*, am creeping through a new one (to prevent myself crying) at odd moments, two or three speeches at a time. I dont know what it is about.'[9] Shaw's claim to have 'written whole plays *d'un seul trait*' was no idle boast; his normal method of composition involved concentrated periods of work in which a full-length major work could be completed in a matter of months. *Heartbreak House*, which took more than a year to write and was revised again in successive rough proofs, clearly caused exceptional problems.[10] It is true that he was much preoccupied with other things at the time, not only the war but the Easter 1916 rebellion in Ireland and its aftermath, which deeply shocked him and involved him in a series of public controversies. (One page of the typescript of *Heartbreak House* has the draft of an appeal against the execution of Roger Casement on its verso.) But, other business apart, Shaw was genuinely uncertain of the form and direction that the play would finally take and the completed text shows signs of this uncertainty.

Captain Shotover was central to the play's conception; the idea of the old sea-captain living in the ship-shaped house was one of the germs from which it developed. The mad/wise, drunken/sober semi-prophetic figure is intended to be the most authoritative Shavian voice in *Heartbreak House*. Throughout the play Shotover is often used as an effective instrument of satire, cutting through conventional social attitudes and pompous euphemisms by his strange piercing directness. Some of his great prophetic outbursts are very powerful. But Shaw was not always successful in finding the right tone for Shotover. One small instance of revision in the typescript may illustrate this unsureness of touch. At the end of Act I, with Shotover at his drawing-board devising lucrative inventions, Hector asks him 'Shall I turn up the lights for you?' Shaw originally had Shotover reply 'No. Only in the darkness is there any light for me.' This he crossed out, presumably because it would have sounded impossibly heavy-handed. Instead he tried an ironic joke: 'No. Money is not made in the light.' But he wanted to keep the impression of the Captain's introspective mood, so he re-wrote it again in its final form: 'No. Give me deeper darkness. Money is not made in the light.'[11] The line seems to misfire as a result – it is neither bitter jest nor symbolic statement but an uneasy compromise between the two. There are equally unsuccessful lines of a similar sort elsewhere in the play. When Mangan in Act III is driven to confess that all he has to live on is 'Travelling expenses. And a trifle of commission', Shotover comments with a sententiousness which makes one wince, 'What more have any of us but travelling expenses for our life's journey' (CP, V, 162). Again the speech was still worse in the original typescript – 'What more have any of us but travelling expenses through a vale of tears.'[12] The attempt to turn repartee into gnomic wisdom is all too inclined to result in pseudo-poetic pseudo-aphorisms.

In *Heartbreak House* Shaw tried to fuse symbolic allegory with his more accustomed mode of social comedy and farce, both at the local level of style and the larger level of structure, and the different dramatic idioms caused problems. Act III, in particular, where the symbolic mode becomes more dominant, shows the lack of coherent structural control. It is well-known that Shaw did not know how to end the play until the Zeppelin raid near his house in Hertfordshire in October 1916 supplied him with an ending. But there are other indications in the final act of his uncertainty of direction. For example, the most enigmatic incident of the play, the announcement of Ellie Dunn's mystical marriage to Shotover, was introduced very late, after a complete draft of the play had been finished. However this scene may be interpreted, it was clearly very important as a climax to the developing relationship of Ellie and Shotover. But as it stands it is almost completely unintegrated into the dramatic action, and it made necessary a re-ordering of the scenes around it which disrupted their continuity. It was at this point in the play that Mangan's political position was originally discovered and discussed. Shaw must have felt that such a passage would come very awkwardly after the announcement of the marriage, and he moved it back to a position between Mangan's revelation that he has no money and the scene in which he offers to undress himself. In the original sequence the Lear-like gesture of stripping had a certain logic coming after the humiliation of being forced to confess his poverty. But as it appears in the final text, coming just after he has been boasting of his political success, the emotional continuity is destroyed. It becomes just one more disconnected unmotivated incident in the series of shocks and surprises that make up the final act.

Heartbreak House is an overcrowded play. Many of Shaw's plays are too long; he very often tried to get in more than a play's-worth into a play. But the overcrowding of *Heartbreak House* is different from the gargantuan expanse of *Man and Superman* or the marathon of *Saint Joan*. In other Shaw plays digressions and diversions are seen to be just that. The main line of the dramatic development is rarely in doubt. But having chosen an uncharacteristically diffuse central focus in *Heartbreak House*, Shaw felt bound to give to each character, each strand of the action, at least one separate climax. We get, for example, a prolonged and progressive set of revelations about Mangan's business dealings, in the vein of the early *Plays Unpleasant*. Each of the multiple love-triangles is given a detailed explication down to the relatively minor relationship of Randall and Lady Utterword. No character is to remain uninvestigated, unexplained; Mazzini Dunn is not the prig he seems to be, Boss Mangan has a Christian name and a heart of sorts, even the kindly mothering Nurse Guinness is revealed as a vindictive termagant. Such revelations are very much in the Shavian tradition, but jostling one another as they do in *Heartbreak House* they become all but impossible to take in. Our sense of confusion in reading or watching the play does not come from any obscurity in the handling of the several dramatic episodes. Much of the dialogue has Shaw's usual crispness and clarity, his superb precision of timing. It is, indeed, the very controlled finish of each Shavian scene which leaves us with a sense of the dislocation of one scene from another and prevents that merging of disparate images and emotions which makes for Chekhovian dramatic unity.

For many recent critics *Heartbreak House* represents a new departure for Shaw both in form and mood. This was not the way it appeared to reviewers when the play was first published in 1919. An unsigned review in the *TLS*, probably by Shaw's old friend/enemy, A. B. Walkley, strikes a note sounded by other critics as well:

> After the war Mr Shaw comes back to us unchanged, like an *émigré* returning home after the French Revolution. He has learnt nothing and forgotten nothing. You take up the familiar squat volume in the familiar greenish-grey binding, and find the inside familiar, too: the old point of view, the old logic, the old people, and the old preface.[13]

The Preface to *Heartbreak House*, in particular, might well have seemed like more of the old familiar Shaw. It is a polemic about the war, in its way as fine a polemic as Shaw ever wrote. But the argument as to the origins and significance of the war is constructed on well-established Shavian premises. Central to his attack on the phenomenon of Heartbreak House, 'cultured, leisured Europe before the war', is the Fabian disapproval of the apolitical and uncommitted. The need for educated and cultured people to act on their social and political responsibilities was a doctrine which Shaw preached in and out of season throughout his life. The inhabitants of Heartbreak House were all the more culpable in failing to provide leadership because it left the country governed by the Philistines of Horseback Hall. The war had provided a cataclysmic sense of urgency to the need for Englishmen to learn Captain Shotover's art of navigation: 'Learn it and live; or leave it and be damned' (CP, V, 177). But the demand for social responsibility involved was one of the most fundamental of Shavian tenets. At a deeper ideological level, Shaw ingeniously identifies as a root cause of the war his old enemy, Darwinism. In 'banishing mind from the universe', in setting up as a model of evolutionary progress a purposeless and amoral principle of natural selection by the survival of the fittest, Darwin prepared the way for the might as right competition of imperial powers culminating in the war. Once again Shaw's historical analysis, though it is a response to the new and terrible events of 1914–18, interprets those events in the light of an unchanged intellectual perspective. There is a fierceness of tone in Shaw's denunciation of the war unlike anything in his work before, but the basic outlook remains the same.

It is nearly always misleading to read a Shaw preface as an introduction to the play it prefaces, but never more so than with *Heartbreak House*. Reading the Preface, written in 1919, the play is seen unequivocally as a play about the war. By entitling the Preface 'Heartbreak House and Horseback Hall', Shaw suggests a central focus on the two equally inadequate sections of English upper-class society who, by their complementary deficiencies, led England to war, or rather failed to lead England away from war. This is an extended gloss on Lady Utterword's speech in Act III, Lady Utterword who here stands as spokesperson for Horseback Hall: 'There are only two classes in good society in England: the equestrian classes and the neurotic classes. It isnt mere convention: everybody can see that the people who hunt are the right people and the people who dont are the wrong ones' (CP, V, 160). But although Lady Utterword represents this view throughout, it is hardly a key issue for most of the play. There is no indication of the war, of course, throughout the first two acts which, in itself, is not to be interpreted as a sign that the play is not concerned with the war. *The Magic Mountain* and *Women in Love* equally contain few references to the war, yet are crucially concerned with it none the less. By misdating its composition 1913–16, Shaw misled some critics into thinking that *Heartbreak House* had been started in peacetime and was overtaken by the war. But although this was incorrect and the whole text was written in the war years 1916–17, the idea for it was conceived in peacetime and in some ways to view it wholly as a war play is to misunderstand it.

It is above all to misunderstand Heartbreak House itself. The Preface prepares us for a satiric, a diagnostic analysis of the shortcomings of the highly cultured but aimless Edwardian intelligentsia. The tone of the Preface is extremely bitter:

> Heartbreak House, in short, did not know how to live, at which point all that was left to it was the boast that at least it knew how to die: a melancholy accomplishment which the outbreak of war presently gave it practically unlimited opportunities of displaying. Thus were the firstborn of Heartbreak House smitten; and the young, the innocent, the hopeful expiated the folly and worthlessness of their elders. (CP, v, 22)

So Shaw in 1919, writing out of the terrible anger of having seen so many young men, friends and the children of friends, maimed and killed by what he regarded as an avoidable disaster. But the futile love-making and flute-playing country-house set is not by any means the whole of Heartbreak House as we see it in the play, nor is Shaw's attitude towards it wholly critical or satiric. It is Ellie who names it in Act III – 'this silly house, this strangely happy house, this agonizing house, this house without foundations. I shall call it Heartbreak House' (CP, v, 171). There is ambiguity in this formulation, and there is enough ambiguity in the effect Heartbreak House has on its visitors to make it necessary to identify it as something other than 'cultured, leisured Europe' responsible for the war.

The house is a strange and an estranging environment. Throughout the first act almost all the characters, even the Captain whose house it is, comment on its oddity and disorienting disorder. But the estrangement it effects on the visitors is seen in at least partly positive terms. Ellie and Mangan are the two main characters who develop or are changed under the impact of Heartbreak House and whose development the play's action traces. Ellie we see moving by a process of accelerated emotional growth from youthful innocence through cynical disillusionment to a new if tenuous ideal of 'life with a blessing'. By contrast Mangan is progressively stripped of his pretences of dignity and power, reduced to a whimpering soul annihilated by the bomb-blast from Heaven. The experience of Heartbreak House is purgatorial in that it redeems the redeemable; but it also tests and finds wanting the irredeemable, the damned. In so far as it has this function of soul-making and soul-destroying, Heartbreak House cannot be seen in the simple satiric terms which the play's Preface sets up.

In the Preface Shaw speaks with characteristic contempt of the amorous propensities of the Heartbreakers:

> They took the only part of our society in which there was leisure for high culture, and made it an economic, political, and, as far as practicable, a moral vacuum; and as Nature, abhorring the vacuum, immediately filled it up with sex and with all sorts of refined pleasures, it was a very delightful place at its best for moments of relaxation. (CP, v, 14)

In the play he introduces an elaborate series of interlocking love-triangles – Shotover:Ellie:Mangan; Mangan:Hesione:Hector; Hector:Ellie:Hesione; Hector:Ariadne:Randall – to illustrate such refined diversions. But the effect of these love-tangles in action is not quite what one would expect. To start with, for all his talk of Nature filling up the vacuum with sex, Shaw shows his usual squeamishness about portraying real sexual attachments. In the original typescript, there were ironically innocent indications from Ellie that Mangan had tried seduction before offering to marry her, and Randall was fairly unmistakeably Lady Utterword's lover.[14] Such references were cut and in the final version sex as distinct from love-talk does not figure at all. This could be interpreted as a further comment on the futility of the Heartbreakers' romancing – as Hector says contemptuously when Randall explains that his relationship with Lady Utterword is Platonic, 'She makes you her servant; and when pay-day comes round, she bilks you' (CP, v, 156). But it gives to the love-relationships an air of unconvincing unreality. If something like the atmosphere of Bloomsbury were to be taken as a real-life counterpart for Heartbreak House – and Shaw did stay at a country-house with Virginia and Leonard Woolf while working on the play and long afterwards remembered it as a significant meeting[15] – then the lack of sexual activity in the Shavian characters' lives does seem a remarkable gap.

Shaw could never bring himself to believe in romantic love as other than infatuation. The typical technique of the *Plays Pleasant*, for instance, was to cure the characters of such infatuation and teach them to found their relationships on a more substantial basis. In *Heartbreak House*, also, the pangs of disappointed love are intended, at least in the case of Ellie, to make possible a deeper form of fulfilment. 'I, Ellie Dunn, give my broken heart and my strong sound soul to its natural captain, my spiritual husband and second father' (CP, v, 168). The broken heart does not impair the soul; if anything it makes possible a new understanding of the nature of the soul. Puritan and Platonist that he was, Shaw saw sexual attraction as an illusory stage in a progress upward towards a higher love. But with this firm sense of the illusory nature of romantic passion, the reality of the central concept of *Heartbreak House* is called in question. Desmond MacCarthy, as so often one of the most perceptive of Shaw's critics, put the point forcibly in his 1921 review of the play: 'Mr Shaw does not know what heartbreak is. He conceives it as a sudden disillusionment (*vide* his heroine), cauterising like a flash of lightning; as a sharp pain, but not as a maiming misery.'[16] We cannot take Ellie's daydream romance with Hector Hushabye very seriously because Shaw himself does not, and it is correspondingly hard to treat her disenchantment as the devastating emotional experience which it is supposed to be – killing a whole part of her life, 'the best part that can never come again' (CP, v, 123).

'Damn braces; bless relaxes' might have been one of Shaw's favourite Blakean aphorisms. Ellie's reaction to her discovery of Hector's real identity as Hesione's husband is for Shaw an exemplary one:

> *Mrs Hushabye* [*laying Ellie down at the end of the sofa*]: Now, pettikins, he is gone. Theres nobody but me. You can let yourself go. Dont try to control yourself. Have a good cry.
> *Ellie* [*raising her head*]: Damn! (CP, v, 84)

If the representation of love was a problematic area in Shaw's drama, the representation of grief is non-existent. In his own life Shaw seems to have defended himself against the experience of grief by either laughter or anger. His behaviour at his mother's funeral provoked Granville Barker to remark, 'You certainly are a merry fellow.'[17] But even more striking is his letter to Mrs Patrick Campbell replying to the news of her son's death in action in 1918: 'It is no use: I cant be sympathetic: these things simply make me furious. I want to swear. I *do* swear. Killed just because people are blasted fools.'[18] The letter ends as it begins in a passion of anger which was Shaw's sincerest form of sympathy. The dumb and hopeless misery of desolation and loss appears to have been outside Shaw's temperamental range and it is outside the range of his drama. The dynamic reaction of anger, if only the anger of self-reproach exemplified by Ellie damning herself for having been such a fool, might always provide a therapeutic antidote to grief.

Heartbreak House has been seen as the despairing indictment of the house's inhabitants whose feckless futility doomed Europe to war, but it does not despair of the Heartbreakers as a whole. For Ellie, the visitor to the house, there may be a spiritual stage beyond despair in her mystical union with the Captain, but for those who live in Heartbreak House there is some hope too, or at least some sympathy. Both of the Hushabyes are depicted with a degree of attractiveness and apparent Shavian approval which makes it impossible to comprehend them within a wholesale satiric critique of the atmosphere of the house. Hesione, one of the finest mature women's parts that Shaw ever created, is a character of enormous charm and real good will in her efforts to extricate Ellie from the clutches of Boss Mangan. She uses her charm unscrupulously but selflessly in Ellie's interests and, though we may sense a degree of Shavian criticism of her restless sophistication, the overwhelming impression is of a human warmth which attracted Shaw himself. Hector Hushabye is an ageing latter-day Sergius, yet he does not receive Sergius's purely comic treatment. There is something pitiable and grotesque in this real man of action reduced to a domestic pet who sublimates his energies in fantasy and philandering. More significantly, and somewhat surprisingly, Hector is given a key role in articulating what are identifiably Shavian principles in conversation with Shotover. The Captain proposes extermination for people like Mangan and Randall Utterword: 'There is enmity between our seed and their seed. They know it and act on it, strangling our souls. They believe in themselves. When we believe in ourselves, we shall kill them' (CP, v, 100–1). But Hector reminds him, with one of Shaw's favourite quotations, that 'we are members one of another', and that to destroy 'their' seed is to destroy 'ours' also. Here and elsewhere in the play Hector advances a version of Shaw's ideal of Creative Evolution, even though in the new context of war it is only as an alternative to extinction: 'Either out of that darkness some new creation will come to supplant us as we have supplanted the animals, or the heavens will fall in thunder and destroy us' (CP, v, 159).

For all Shaw's diatribes in the Preface against the failure of responsibility of the Heartbreakers, his sympathies remained with them. *Heartbreak House* is a partisan play. When it came to the horrors of war and war fever, Shaw was necessarily allied with the liberal intellectuals of Heartbreak House against the Philistines represented by Mangan, Randall or Sir Hastings Utterword, indeed more whole-heartedly with them than ever before. Hector as much as Shotover identifies them as the enemy: 'I must believe that my spark, small as it is, is divine, and that the red light over their door is hell fire' (CP, v, 101). It is Mangan who is the key figure in this company of the damned, Mangan who came to represent what Shaw most hated in the English conduct of the war. Mangan's real-life counterpart, Lord Devonport, was made food minister in Lloyd George's 'business cabinet' at the end of 1916 and the appointment clearly infuriated Shaw, not only because it was undemocratic – Mangan boasts at having been asked to 'join the Government without even going through the nonsense of an election' (CP, v, 163) – but because it showed what he regarded as a misplaced belief in the ability of 'practical business men'. Their failure, he maintained in the Preface to *Heartbreak House*, 'proved not only that they were useless for public work, but that in a well-ordered nation they would never have been allowed to control private enterprise' (CP, v, 38).

Mangan has less to recommend him than any other Shaw character since Sir George Crofts in *Mrs Warren's Profession*. He is Shaw's most wholly polemic portrait of the capitalist. It is as though Mangan was conceived as the antithesis of Undershaft, the capitalist idealised. Undershaft was a model employer and passionately involved in the business of making armaments: Mangan is not concerned with his employees or the products of his factories: as Mazzini Dunn reveals, 'He never goes near the men: he

couldnt manage them: he is afraid of them. I never can get him to
take the least interest in the works' (CP, v, 116). His only interest,
his only aptitude is for what Marx called the generation of 'surplus
value', the pure drive of capital to make more capital. He is
nicknamed Boss but the final revelation is that he is in no sense a
boss, he does not even make money for himself but for a syndicate of
which he is only a tool. Shaw's dislike of Mangan comes out in the
unusually vituperative introductory description:

> Mangan, carefully frock-coated as for church or for a director's
> meeting, is about fiftyfive, with a careworn, mistrustful expres-
> sion, standing a little on an entirely imaginary dignity, with a
> dull complexion, straight, lustreless hair, and features so entirely
> commonplace that it is impossible to describe them. (CP, v, 86).

In the context of Heartbreak House he is the real outsider, mocked
at, despised, regarded as physically and morally either ludicrous or
repulsive, and though Shaw allows him moments at which we may
sympathise with his humiliation, by and large he invites us to share
the attitudes of the other characters towards him. The antipathy to
Mangan is so general that it aligns virtually the whole cast against
him. In Act III as he prepares, not for the first time, to storm out in a
huff, he is mocked by a chorus of voices:

> *Mrs Hushabye*: Goodbye, Alf. Think of us sometimes in the city.
>   Think of Ellie's youth!
> *Ellie*: Think of Hesione's eyes and hair!
> *Captain Shotover*: Think of this garden in which you are not a dog
>   barking to keep the truth out!
> *Hector*: Think of Lady Utterword's beauty! her good sense! her
>   style! (CP, v, 167)

Elsewhere Heartbreak House may be opposed to Lady Utterword's
Horseback Hall, Shotover's truth-telling may stand against the
delusions of his demon daughters, but here they represent together
an image of self-consciousness, intelligence and charm from which
Mangan is ruthlessly excluded.

In a letter to his Swedish translator Hugo Vallentin, Shaw said
that *Heartbreak House* 'seems to me a fine opening spoilt by the war
and by Lord Devonport (Mangan)'.[19] Mangan upset the balance of
sympathy within the play by the degree of Shaw's reaction against

his real-life original; the war created an emotional atmosphere in which it was extremely difficult to achieve artistic detachment. In the Preface, Shaw explained that he had to withhold the play during the war itself because 'Truth telling is not compatible with the defence of the realm . . . comedy, though sorely tempted, had to be loyally silent; for the art of the dramatic poet knows no patriotism; recognises no obligation but truth to natural history' (CP, v, 58). This is consistent with the assumption of the Preface that *Heartbreak House* is a satiric comedy telling the severe truth about the war and the mental attitudes that caused it. In fact the play has a much less controlled, a much more reactive relation to the war than that. The incident of the Zeppelin crashing near Ayot St Lawrence provided the otherwise unforeseen ending, but the whole mood of the play's final act involved the mixed emotions generated by the experience of the war.

Mrs Hushabye is the first to hear the 'sort of splendid drumming in the sky' at the beginning of Act III and Hector interprets it as 'Heaven's threatening growl of disgust at us useless futile creatures' (CP, v, 159). Shaw prepares us for the air-raid specifically as an image of apocalypse. Ringing denunciations of Heartbreak House and its people come from Hector and from Shotover:

> *Hector*: And this ship that we are all in? This soul's prison we call England?
> *Captain Shotover*: The captain is in his bunk, drinking bottled ditch-water; and the crew is gambling in the forecastle. She will strike and sink and split. Do you think the laws of God will be suspended in favor of England because you were born in it? (CP, v, 177).

At the personal spiritual level a resolution is offered in the union of Ellie and the Captain, but such personal fulfilment is not enough, as Shotover makes clear: 'I tell you happiness is no good. You can be happy when you are only half alive. I am happier now I am half dead than ever I was in my prime' (CP, v, 169). There remains a judgement on the half-dead Heartbreak House, apathetic, irresponsible, squandering its talents and its gifts. 'We have been too long here. We do not live in this house. We haunt it' (CP, v, 171).

In this context, the response to the Zeppelin attack is one of wild excitement:

Mrs Hushabye: . . . Did you hear the explosions? And the sound in the sky: it's like an orchestra: it's like Beethoven.
Ellie: By thunder, Hesione: it is Beethoven. (CP, v, 178)

This could be interpreted as the final symptom of the moral degeneracy of the Heartbreakers, their willingness to see apocalypse as the ultimate aesthetic phenomenon, a welcome stimulus for jaded appetites. There is indeed a terrible irony in the famous ending:

Mrs Hushabye: But what a glorious experience! I hope theyll come again tomorrow night.
Ellie [*radiant at the prospect*]: Oh, I hope so. (CP, v, 181)

But in giving Ellie this concluding line Shaw was drawing on his own experience. 'What is hardly credible, but true, is that the sound of the Zepp's engines was so fine, and its voyage through the stars so enchanting, that I positively caught myself hoping next night that there would be another raid.'[20] Shaw was ashamed at the lack of concern in his response, but it is a relatively innocent feeling and there is very little sense of critical condemnation in the evocation of equivalent feelings in the play. On the contrary, we are stirred by the triumphant recklessness with which the attack is regarded, Hesione and Ellie's excitement, Lady Utterword's imperious calm, Hector's bravado as he defies the blackout order: 'There is not half light enough. We should be blazing to the skies' (CP, v, 179). The Captain sums up the mood: 'The judgement has come. Courage will not save you; but it will shew that your souls are still alive' (CP, v, 179). But courage does save them and dooms to death the two cowards who went to hide in the gravel-pit. The dynamite which the Captain had been keeping 'to kill fellows like Mangan' does its job after all. The destruction of Mangan and the burglar, the two characters beyond redemption, confirms the impression that we are intended to see the rest of the cast as saved or capable of salvation.

The emotion experienced by those in Heartbreak House at the Zeppelin raid is more akin to the feeling of 1914 than it is to 1916–17, the period of the play's composition. It was not only Rupert Brooke who felt at the beginning of the war – 'Now, God be thanked Who has matched us with His hour.' Any number of writers, including some who were later to prove the war's most bitter critics such as Robert Graves and Siegfried Sassoon, testify to this emotion of relief and release of August 1914. There is a conflict in the play between real time and allegorical time. With the Zeppelin raid Shaw apparently dated the action of *Heartbreak House* in wartime. But in so far as the play provides an image of 'cultured, leisured Europe before the war', and the air-raid in the last act is apparently quite unexpected, it figures instead the outbreak of the war. This accounts for the lack of verisimilitude of which Desmond MacCarthy complains:

> As a picture of behaviour and talk in an English country house during the summer of nineteen-fifteen or sixteen or seventeen, or whenever the action is supposed to take place, the play has no relation to reality. . . . Neither the denizens of *Heartbreak House*, nor those of Horseback Hall, behaved like the characters in this play when the catastrophe came.[21]

We need not take the play at quite this literal level, but rather as a symbolic representation of upper-class England facing into the war, though with the hindsight of what the war was to be like. As such it operates not so much as a dramatic image of apocalypse in action but rather as a warning of catastrophe to come.

This is not, I think, a merely technical distinction. For all Shaw's horror at the war, at the hysteria and the rhetorical patriotic lies at home and the hideously costly blunders of the front, he continued to believe at some level that there were lessons to be learned from it which *could* be learned. *Heartbreak House* is not a play of despair. We see particularly in Hector the dawning consciousness of the cost of irresponsibility by him and his kind:

> We sit here talking, and leave everything to Mangan and to chance and to the devil. Think of the powers of destruction that Mangan and his mutual admiration gang wield! It's madness: it's like giving a torpedo to a badly brought up child to play at earthquakes with. (CP, v, 175)

Shotover's desire to reach the 'seventh degree of concentration' is not representative of a purely mystical introspection – Shaw changed the original phrase 'seventh degree of contemplation' perhaps because it suggested this sort of inwardness.[22] Instead it symbolises the need to harness thought and will to action, to combat the dangerous stupidity of those who hold the powers of destruction. The war may have brought home to Shaw the terrible dangers of the

Undershaft armament factories if they were not controlled by the hypothetical trio of Undershaft, Cusins and Barbara, but he still believed potently in the need to bring them under such control. Of this Shotover's thought-ray, which can explode his enemy's dynamite, is emblem. Such will to survive as is to be found in *Heartbreak House* is under extreme threat both from inertia within and a mindless destructiveness without, but it is there none the less. If man will learn the art of navigation, even in these latter days, he may live.

The idea of apocalypse was the power-house for much of the greatest Modernist literature; it is there in Yeats, Eliot and Lawrence. Shaw had not that sort of delight in the imagination of disaster and *Heartbreak House* is in fact a far cry from 'The Second Coming', *The Waste Land* or *Women in Love*. Still less does it resemble *King Lear*, the greatest of all apocalyptic works with which Shaw himself compared it. The war moved Shaw to intense anger, at times to weary depression, but never to tragic despair. The mood of *Heartbreak House* includes a reaction of disgust against the Heartbreakers' futile love-charades, a real sense of the doom towards which their aimlessness may be heading, but there is still a stubborn and characteristic strain of optimism which will not let the play settle into tragedy. There is much to admire and enjoy in *Heartbreak House*, the conception of characters such as Shotover or Hesione Hushabye, the vitality of comic dialogue, the composition of individual scenes, but the very best effects in it work against its coherence as a play of mood and symbol. Shaw's typical modes of discussion-comedy, extravaganza and farce keep disrupting the integrated atmosphere and symbolic design. In so far as *Heartbreak House* may be seen as an attempt to find a new poetic/allegorical form to explore the spiritual *malaise* which led to the war, then it must be considered a play only very partially successful because written against the Shavian grain.

9 Shavian History

There is a story (apocryphal no doubt) of a Cecil B. de Mille epic in which the troops were roused by the stirring line, 'Men of the Middle Ages, let us now rise up and go out and fight the Hundred Years War'. Anachronism is of the essence in any dramatisation of history. We can only see what we can from where we are. To us the Middle Ages are the Middle Ages, after the Dark Ages, before the Renaissance; however little aware the soldiers at Crécy or Poitiers were of the fact, we know that the war they were fighting was to last on and off for roughly a hundred years. To ask modern actors to play the parts of historical figures, to write for them lines which will be intelligible to contemporary audiences, to make of the complicated and half-known facts of the past an immediate and dramatic present, is and must be anachronism enacted. Indeed, one of the commonest forms of inauthenticity in historical drama derives from a superficial concern with the accurate recreation of period. Scrupulously faithful costumes and décor, careful historical background research, can often do no more than make us aware that what we are watching is a shell of past action conspicuously empty of reality. If the history play or film is going to convince us, it must create its own reality which lives in our here and now.

But with the greatest history plays – and in English this means Shakespeare and nobody else – there is a profound sense of an encounter with the past. We all know the jokes about the conspirators in *Julius Caesar* with their very un-Roman hats plucked down over their faces. Yet T. S. Eliot was surely right when he argued that 'Shakespeare acquired more essential history from Plutarch than most men could from the whole British Museum'.[1] The Roman tragedies are very much plays of their own time, but they represent a vision of Roman history which is not merely a projection backwards of Renaissance England. There is in *Coriolanus* a vivid evocation of the atmosphere of the emergent Republic, in *Julius Caesar* and *Antony and Cleopatra* a compelling view of the power politics through which the Republic was turned into the Empire.

Whether or not they represent historical truth, the plays show us Shakespeare's imagination inhabiting a milieu which is identifiably not his own, reaching out to a past which he authenticates by his capacity to imagine it.

Shaw in *Saint Joan* measured himself against Shakespeare, not obtrusively and aggressively as in *Caesar and Cleopatra*, but without diffidence either. In the Preface he explained his procedure in conceiving the historical characters who surrounded Joan:

> I really knew no more about these men and their circle than Shakespear knew about Falconbridge and the Duke of Austria, or about Macbeth and Macduff. In view of the things they did in history, and have to do again in the play, I can only invent appropriate characters for them in Shakespear's manner. (CP, VI, 70)

But, he went on to claim, he was in a position to understand the medieval period as Shakespeare, living still too close to it in time, never could. That understanding, moreover, was an understanding of the significance of historical events which, he complained, Shakespeare never attempted: 'a novice can read his plays from one end to the other without learning that the world is finally governed by forces expressing themselves in religions and laws which make epochs rather than by vulgarly ambitious individuals who make rows' (CP, VI, 70–1). His *Saint Joan* was to be more than a Shakespearean clash of characters, much more than a conventional costume drama:

> Those who see it performed will not mistake the startling result it records for a mere personal accident. They will have before them not only the visible and human puppets, but the Church, the Inquisition, the Feudal System, with divine inspiration always beating against their too inelastic limits: all more terrible in their dramatic force than any of the little mortal figures clanking about in plate armor or moving silently in the frocks and hoods of the order of St Dominic. (CP, VI, 71)

Shaw's object was to write a play in which what he took to be the historical significance of the life of the fifteenth-century saint would be manifest to a twentieth-century audience. What sort of dramatic reality was the result?

One answer is supplied in the Preface, where Shaw speaks of *Saint Joan* as showing 'the romance of her rise, the tragedy of her execution, and the comedy of the attempts of posterity to make amends for that execution' (CP, VI, 66). The play is in turn romance, tragedy and comedy, the three modes corresponding to its three movements: scenes I–III concerned with the rise of Joan up to the climax of the relief of the siege of Orléans; scenes IV–VI showing not only the trial and execution but the chain of circumstances which led up to it; and the Epilogue which evokes the five-hundred-year-long rehabilitation which ended with Joan's canonisation in 1920.[2] To try to define the quality of *Saint Joan* we need to consider the nature of these three modes and movements and how far they blend together to give us something which is both genuinely Shaw and genuinely a play about Joan of Arc.

Again and again in the Preface and elsewhere, Shaw stressed that in writing the play he had done no more than dramatise the transcript of her trial and the later fifteenth-century enquiry which reversed the trial's verdict: 'I took the only documents that are of the smallest value – the report of the process and that of the rehabilitation. I simply arranged what I found there for the stage, relying on Joan to pull me through, which she did'.[3] This is, of course, Shavian overstatement but Brian Tyson has made clear how very closely Shaw did stick to his main source, T. Douglas Murray's edited and translated version of J. E. J. Quicherat's *Procès de Jeanne d'Arc*.[4] In returning to the original documents, in rejecting the romantic legends which had grown up about Joan, Shaw felt that he could realise upon the stage the much more dramatic drama of the real-life events.

To a large extent, therefore, even the romance of Joan's rise to power which is represented in the first three scenes of the play is intended to be anti-romantic romance. Joan, Shaw stresses, was not good-looking, not the beautiful Maid of perfervid imagination. Taking as his model instead the head of St Maurice in Orléans, reputedly a portrait of Joan, he describes her as having 'an uncommon face: eyes very wide apart and bulging as they often do in very imaginative people, a long well-shaped nose with wide nostrils, a short upper lip, resolute but full-lipped mouth, and handsome fighting chin' (CP, VI, 85). Jeanne, from Lorraine in the North of France, in Shaw becomes a rough-speaking country girl with a somewhat dubious North-country dialect. Most annoyingly, and most unconvincingly, Shaw gives to Joan the mannerism which he so frequently gives to his masterful young women, that of calling the other characters by nicknames. Just as Octavius Robinson and Roebuck Ramsden are Ann's Tavy and Granny, as Adolphus Cusins and Charles Lomax become Barbara's Salvation Army recruits Dolly and Cholly, so Joan makes a Jack of Sieur Jean de Metz, a Polly of Bertrand de Poulengy, and a Charlie of the Dauphin. The more resounding the name, the more Shaw delights in reducing it to a nursery-like familiarity which bespeaks the effortless and humiliating control exercised by his strong heroines.

Throughout Shaw is bent on demystifying the figure of Joan. She is to be seen as plain-speaking, buoyant, unabashed, unreverent. Shaw could never conceive 'a great man as a grave man' (CL, II, 180), and his Saint Joan, as much as his Caesar, was to have little time for conventional gravity. But Eric Bentley is exactly right when he claims that Shaw's intention was not only to 'show Joan as a credible human being' but to 'make her *greatness* credible'.[5] He was determined to remove the glamour of the legendary Joan because by making her apparently ordinary, he could all the more effectively highlight what was truly extraordinary in her character – the energy, the resolution, the unswerving will. Throughout the first three scenes of the play, the romance section, we see her steadily imposing her will on others. Robert de Baudricourt, her first and easiest victim, is characterised as 'handsome and physically energetic, but with no will of his own' and when the play opens he 'is disguising that defect in his usual fashion by storming terribly at his steward' (CP, VI, 81). The unfortunate steward, with his deficient hens, is there to represent the bottom of a heap which Joan will swiftly climb to the top. In the second scene her success is all the more remarkable because it is the Dauphin, with his tenacious instinct for survival by the line of least resistance, whom she must inspire with her fighting spirit. There is a significant replay in the interview between Joan and the Dauphin of the encounter between Caesar and Cleopatra. Just as Caesar taught Cleopatra queenliness, Joan, by a similar mixture of harrying and coaxing, gives the Dauphin a crash-course in kingliness. Both are lessons in the use of the will. But the reversal of roles, by which it is the adolescent girl who teaches the older man, makes Joan's achievement all the more striking and enforces Shaw's point that the vital genius, the figure of outstanding will, may appear in any human shape or form.

In the opening scenes of the play Shaw thus goes far towards establishing Joan as an anti-romantic Shavian superwoman. Yet he does not altogether deny to the audience the Maid of romance with her voices and miracles. The voices were clearly a problem for Shaw, as he made clear in the Preface:

> I cannot believe, nor, if I could, could I expect all my readers to believe, as Joan did, that three ocularly visible well dressed persons, named respectively Saint Catherine, Saint Margaret, and Saint Michael, came down from heaven and gave her certain instructions with which they were charged by God for her. Not that such a belief would be more improbable or fantastic than some modern beliefs which we all swallow; but there are fashions and family habits in belief, and it happens that, my fashion being Victorian and my family habit Protestant, I find myself unable to attach any such objective validity to the form of Joan's visions. (CP, VI, 27)

Shaw accordingly interpreted the voices as 'the dramatisation by Joan's imagination of that pressure upon her of the driving force that is behind evolution' (CP, VI, 28). In the opening scene he shows Joan herself aware of this interpretation:

> *Joan*: I hear voices telling me what to do. They come from God.
> *Robert*: They come from your imagination.
> *Joan*: Of course. That is how the messages of God come to us. (CP, VI, 92)

And later she admits that they may be 'only echoes of my own commonsense' (CP, VI, 152). But there can be little doubt that Jeanne d'Arc believed in her communication with the saints at a much more literal level than this. At her trial attempts were made to suggest that she suffered from hallucinations brought about by fasting, or even perhaps from erotic fantasies which might be the sign of demonic possession (as in the authentic question, which Shaw borrows, about whether St Michael appeared to her as a naked man), but Jeanne countered them all with solidly detailed testimony as to the nature of her supernatural visitations. There is an uneasy tension within *Saint Joan* between the representation of the historical Joan's real belief in her voices and Shaw's desire to credit her with something more like his own rationalistic attitude.

Shaw's treatment of Joan's miracles is even more ambiguous, and in some ways less defensible. The Archbishop of Rheims in the second scene gives a non-miraculous account of miracles. He explains to La Trémouille in advance that Joan will be able to spot the substitution of Gilles de Rais for the Dauphin: 'She will know what everybody in Chinon knows: that the Dauphin is the meanest-looking and worst-dressed figure in the Court, and that the man with the blue beard is Gilles de Rais' (CP, VI, 105). But this, he goes on to add, will not make it any less of a miracle.

> A miracle, my friend, is an event which creates faith. That is the purpose and nature of miracles. They may seem very wonderful to the people who witness them, and very simple to those who perform them. That does not matter: if they confirm or create faith they are true miracles. (CP, VI, 105)

This concept of the miracle as a faith-creating conjuring trick might seem to be Shaw's own. Several critics have assumed that we are not intended to accept Joan's miracles at their face value, but instead to witness their effect on those more credulous than ourselves. However, when we consider the dramatic use to which the miracles are put, it is hard to sustain this view.

The miracle of the eggs in the first scene was, as Shaw himself explained, an invention to take the place of the real event which convinced or converted Robert de Baudricourt:

> The apparent miracle which impressed him was the news of the Battle of Herrings. Joan learnt this from the mouth to mouth wireless of the peasantry. She was therefore able to tell him what had happened several days before the news reached him by the official routine of mounted messenger. This seemed to him miraculous. A much simpler form of miracle has been substituted in the play to save tedious and unnecessary explanations. (CP, VI, 212–13)

In giving a sceptical explanation of the real-life 'miracle' here, Shaw would seem to imply that the invented substitute is of a similar order. But this is hardly the effect of the strong ending of the first scene:

> *The steward runs in with a basket.*
> *Steward*: Sir, sir –
> *Robert*: What now?
> *Steward*: The hens are laying like mad, sir. Five dozen eggs!

> *Robert* [*stiffens convulsively; crosses himself; and forms with his pale lips the words*]: Christ in heaven! [*Aloud but breathless*] She did come from God. (CP, VI, 96)

This is pure ham, but it is surely unironic ham, intended to send shivers of excitement up the spine in the theatre. Similarly with the changing of the wind before Orléans in scene III.

> *Dunois* [*looking at the pennon*]: The wind has changed. [*He crosses himself*] God has spoken. [*Kneeling and handing his baton to Joan*] You command the king's army. I am your soldier. (CP, VI, 122–3)

In performance it is impossible to respond at this moment with sceptical detachment, to smile at Dunois's naiveté (he is not naive) in seeing supernatural meaning in a natural event. To claim that Shaw, at moments like these, is 'satirising popular religious psychology'[6] is like the neo-classical critics who defended Homer's (otherwise improper) inclusion of the marvellous in *The Odyssey* by explaining that all those stories of the Cyclops and the Sirens were simply fantasies invented by Odysseus for the benefit of the gullible Phaeacians.

Each of the first three scenes of *Saint Joan* ends with a similar high-point, as the miracles of the Maid create faith in those around her. The audience is surely intended to share this excitement. And yet at some level we must be affected by Shaw's partial scepticism, his awareness that what he is writing is 'romance'. Sybil Thorndike recounts how when Shaw first read the play to her, after she had listened spell-bound to the opening three scenes, he remarked 'That's all flapdoodle up to there – just "theatre" to get you interested – now the play begins'.[7] One suspects that the comment may have been partly a matter of embarrassment at the romantic nature of these scenes, but there is nevertheless a damning ring of truth to it. The romance section of the play is skilfully crafted – Shaw had not worked in the theatre for thirty years for nothing – but, with its blend of farcical comedy and drama, its atmospheric kingfishers on the Loire, it seems often more a knowing exploitation of theatricality than an action of real dramatic integrity.

And Shaw's real business does begin in scene IV. The tent-scene is a brilliant and wholly Shavian invention which is crucial to the play's structure. It gives Joan herself a much-needed break from the stage and in her absence makes possible a broad and generalising discussion of the meaning of her life (and in anticipation) of her death. Shaw chooses for his interlocutors the Earl of Warwick, who commanded the English forces at the time of Joan's capture and execution, and the Bishop of Beauvais who presided over her trial. They represent in this scene the view-point of the feudal nobility and of the Church, as Shaw saw it the two great forces to which Joan was opposed. They are characterised only to the limited extent that they need to be contrasted. It scarcely matters if we agree with Desmond MacCarthy that Warwick 'is a purely eighteenth-century noble-man'.[8] There is no effort made to pretend that Cauchon and Warwick are 'in period' in this scene; rather they self-consciously expound what they are about in a conversation which is necessarily out of normal historical time. The principle involved is the cardinal one for Shaw, advanced in the Preface: 'it is the business of the stage to make its figures more intelligible to themselves than they would be in real life; for by no other means can they be made intelligible to the audience' (CP, VI, 73). The third party to the conversation in the tent-scene, the English chaplain De Stogumber, has been very commonly written off as one of Shaw's mistakes in the play. However irritating we may find Shaw's crude and silly caricature of the chauvinist Englishman, he does to some extent turn that irritation to account by making of De Stogumber the butt of Cauchon and Warwick as well as our butt, by using his clownish interruptions to vary and punctuate the main formal debate.

The purpose of the debate is to establish the essential principles of Protestantism and nationalism for which Shaw claimed Joan stood. In a cleverly choreographed dialogue, Warwick the feudalist and Cauchon the Catholic churchman diagnose the two ideas associated with Joan which they are resolved to combat. On the one hand, as Warwick says, there is 'the protest of the individual soul against the interference of priest or peer between the private man and his God. I should call it Protestantism if I had to find a name for it.' On the other, as Cauchon puts it, for Joan 'the French-speaking people are what the Holy Scriptures describe as a nation. Call this side of her heresy Nationalism if you will' (CP, VI, 139). There were, in-evitably, protests against this interpretation of Shaw's as eccentric and wildly anachronistic, but he had more than a little support for it in his source. He might well have taken his cue for Joan's nationalism from a comment in T. Douglas Murray's Introduction:

Nations in the modern sense had not fully arisen. The State was everything. Whether a great Anglo-French monarchy sitting in Paris ruled over France, England, Ireland, and Wales, or a more domestic French line only ruled over France itself, was a question on which upright men might well take opposite sides. Jeanne's special merit was that she saw the possibility of a great French nation, self-centred, self-sufficient, and she so stamped this message on the French heart that its characters have never faded.[9]

Her 'Protestantism' is illustrated on page after page of the transcript of her trial, as she refused categorically to accept that the Church Militant was a higher authority than her own sense of her divine mission. When she was asked, 'Will you submit your actions and words to the decision of the Church?', she replied, 'My words and deeds are all in God's hands: in all I wait upon him'; or again:

> 'Will you refer yourself to the decision of the Church?'
> 'I refer myself to God Who sent me, to our Lady, and to all the Saints in Paradise. And in my opinion it is all one, God and the Church; and one should make no difficulty about it'.[10]

The rehabilitation enquiry was at pains to try to establish that Joan had been willing to submit her case to the Pope or to a General Council of the Church, refusing to accept the judgement only of the ecclesiastical court which was packed with her political enemies. This was the view, also, of Shaw's friend the Irish priest, Father Leonard, who acted as his 'technical adviser' while he was writing the play.[11] But the occasional references in the trial itself to the possibility of an appeal to the Pope appear to be ambiguous at best, and there is much to support Shaw's reading of Joan as unable to accept any authority which would deny the truth of her personal inspiration by God.

Whether we accept Joan as proto-nationalist, proto-Protestant or not, there is a remarkable detachment in the presentation of the arguments in the tent-scene. Shaw has perhaps relatively little real sympathy for Warwick's point of view, the feudal barons' fear of a centralised monarchy which would break their power deriving from Joan's idea of the king as God's deputy, but Warwick is allowed to present it articulately and with force. But to Cauchon the Catholic Shaw gives real eloquence:

What will the world be like when The Church's accumulated wisdom and knowledge and experience, its councils of learned, venerable pious men, are thrust into the kennel by every ignorant laborer or dairy-maid whom the devil can puff up with the monstrous self-conceit of being directly inspired from heaven? It will be a world of blood, of fury, of devastation, of each man striving for his own hand: in the end a world wrecked back into barbarism. (CP, VI, 135)

With all the 'holy wars' of the Reformation and Counter-Reformation to look back on, not to mention the nationalist conflicts which had culminated in Shaw's day in the First World War, the identification of Joan as Protestant and nationalist was no doubt intended to give us pause. Robert Whitman scarcely puts it too strongly when he says that Shaw's Joan appears as the 'saint of emergent capitalism'.[12] And yet we are made to feel that the attitude of Cauchon and Warwick, however deeply understandable, is a reactionary one, and that the spirit of Joan, however terrible its historical consequences, must be supported against them. Shaw was an internationalist politically, and the medieval idea of a supra-national state and church should have had much to recommend it to him. Elsewhere in his work, most notably in *John Bull's Other Island*, he appeals to a concept of fully catholic Catholicism transcending national barriers as an ultimate ideal. But he resisted the common nineteenth-century socialist tendency to sentimentalise medieval feudalism, and instead celebrated Joan as one of those exceptional historical figures whose mission is to move the world on, even it was to move it on to other terrible eras.

If scene IV shows us the full force of Joan's enemies and what they stood for, scene V gives the equivalent picture of how little support she was to expect from her friends. Just as he left Joan immediately before the triumph of the relief of Orléans, it was a real dramatist's instinct which made Shaw return to her in Rheims cathedral immediately after the great climax of the crowning of the Dauphin. With Joan praying in the empty cathedral, we catch a glimpse of a private moment between two public shows, the coronation and the appearance to the people outside. In this behind the scenes atmosphere, Shaw builds up naturally and effectively the sense of her isolation. Once again the individual characters who warn Joan stand for more than themselves. If she is captured, she will not have the support of the monarchy – Charles will not ransom her; though the Archbishop of Rheims is on her side politically, he will not use the authority of the Church to help her against Cauchon and the Inquisition; Dunois, her closest friend and companion in arms, yet speaks firmly for the army that he will not risk the life of a single soldier to save her. With immense skill Shaw creates out of the individual voices a formal chorus of renunciation.

That chorus is designed to bring out the developing emotions of Joan. She begins in the affectionate intimacy of a conversation with Dunois who, for all his feeling for her, cannot really understand when she tries to tell him about her voices: 'You make me uneasy when you talk about your voices: I should think you were a bit cracked if I hadnt noticed that you give me very sensible reasons for what you do, though I hear you telling others you are only obeying Madame Saint Catherine.' To which Joan can only retort 'crossly', 'Well, I have to find reasons for you, because you do not believe in my voices. But the voices come first; and I find the reasons after: whatever you may choose to believe' (CP, VI, 143). It is almost as though in Dunois Shaw parodied his own inclination to rationalise Joan's voices – he too uses the mocking 'Madame Saint Catherine' in the Preface. The relationship between Joan and Dunois remains an affectionate one, but limited in understanding. When they are joined by the other main characters, Joan makes a rather half-hearted offer to the King to return to her village now her mission to crown him in Rheims has been accomplished, and is visibly hurt and taken aback by the alacrity with which the offer is accepted. She is stung to vociferous and belligerent opposition by talk of treaties and an unwillingness on the part of the French to press home the advantages she has won for them. She attacks the faint-hearts with rough arrogance: 'I tell you, Bastard, your art of war is no use, because your knights are no good for real fighting' (CP, VI, 149). It is only by degrees that she registers the full force of the animus against her and her arguments, and in the rhetorical clash the other voices in the chorus come to dominate hers. She is horrified and bewildered by the threats that are made against her.

And yet out of that horror and bewilderment, out of the realisation that she is alone, she draws the strength which is expressed in one of the greatest speeches in Shaw. It must be quoted at length:

> Yes: I am alone on earth: I have always been alone. My father told my brothers to drown me if I would not stay to mind his sheep

while France was bleeding to death: France might perish if only our lambs were safe. I thought France would have friends at the court of the king of France; and I find only wolves fighting for pieces of her poor torn body. I thought God would have friends everywhere, because He is the friend of everyone; and in my innocence I believed that you who now cast me out would be like strong towers to keep harm from me. But I am wiser now; and nobody is any the worse for being wiser. Do not think you can frighten me by telling me that I am alone. France is alone; and God is alone; and what is my loneliness before the loneliness of my country and my God? I see now that the loneliness of God is his strength: what would He be if He listened to your jealous little counsels? Well, my loneliness shall be my strength too; it is better to be alone with God: His friendship will not fail me, nor His counsel, nor His love. In His strength I will dare, and dare, and dare, until I die. I will not go out now to the common people, and let the love in their eyes comfort me for the hate in yours. You will all be glad to see me burnt; but if I go through the fire I shall go through it to their hearts for ever and ever. And so, God be with me! (CP, VI, 154)

The scriptural echoes of so much of this speech are made all the more effective for the development of the pastoral image from literal to metaphorical level. The two main rhetorical movements are separated by a nicely judged piece of commonsensical colloquialism: 'But I am wiser now; and nobody is any the worse for being wiser.' The touch of childish petulance – 'You will all be glad to see me burnt' – is turned into a ringing affirmation of the meaning of martyrdom. It is here that we truly see what Shaw meant by calling Joan a Protestant. As Brian Tyson has pointed out, the speech draws upon the final lines of Stockmann in *An Enemy of the People*, 'the strongest man in the world is he who stands most alone'.[13] There is a strain of absolute individualism in Ibsen, however hedged round with ironies it may be in the figure of Stockmann, and it is this Protestant individualist stance which Shaw attributes to Joan: 'it is better to be alone with God'.

In the trial-scene Shaw did, very nearly, what he claimed he had done, that is to dramatise and arrange the events, even the very words, which he found in the original documents. Many of the questions and many of Joan's replies are taken all but verbatim from Murray and, though Joan's recantation and subsequent retraction of the recantation happened over a period of days, what Shaw gives is only a theatrically heightened image of what actually took place. The main Shavian invention in the trial-scene is the figure of the Inquisitor and the immensely long speech he is given in defence of his role. Shaw's insistence, against all the traditional prejudices, that the judges who tried Joan were fair-minded and reasonable men is, of course, one of the key features of the play and provoked the most controversy (as no doubt it was intended to do). The Inquisitor's apologia might seem to be the ultimate achievement in Shavian devil's advocacy. Certainly Murray, his main source from whom he derived so much, took the conventional view of the authorities who tried Joan. 'The worst of these servile churchmen was the wretched Bishop of Beauvais, Pierre Cauchon. Many other prelates were Caesar's friends, but he sits exalted in solitary infamy.'[14] Yet it was not merely perversity which made Shaw try to reverse this verdict on Joan's accusers. Reading through the account of the trial and the rehabilitation enquiry, one can see why Shaw saw it as he did. There can be little doubt that the Bishop of Beauvais, as supporter of the English, under constant pressure to find Jeanne guilty, must have to some extent been biased against her. Yet the trial lasted over three months, Jeanne was very comprehensively examined and frequently exhorted to repent, and though some anecdotal evidence suggests that Cauchon was determined to find a means to convict her even after the recantation, there is also a suggestion – on which Shaw built – that he refused to act merely as an ecclesiastical stooge for the English. It was not a kangaroo-court that tried Jeanne d'Arc; if it was, obviously, in some sense a political trial, the rehabilitation proceedings were every bit as political, perhaps more evidently bent on redeeming the reputation of Jeanne than the original judges were on convicting her.

Shaw acknowledged in the Preface that he flattered the character of Cauchon, virtually invented the character of the Inquisitor, who is a very shadowy figure in the account of the trial. But he argues that such were the 'inevitable flatteries of tragedy', that in order to make the trial of Joan fully significant, he had to make her judges the best possible representatives of the system that found her guilty:

> It is, I repeat, what normally innocent people do that concerns us; and if Joan had not been burnt by normally innocent people in the energy of their righteousness her death at their hands would have no more significance than the Tokyo earthquake, which burnt a great many maidens. The tragedy of such murders is that

they are not committed by murderers. They are judicial murders, pious murders; and this contradiction at once brings an element of comedy into the tragedy. (CP, VI, 72)

This is a very significant passage. It is typical of Shaw in his refusal to be interested in evil, his belief that most of what is wrong in the world is caused by misguided people acting according to their lights. It explains why he lavishes on Cauchon and the Inquisitor such evident sincerity, such reasoning force and eloquence. They are serious men who fervently believe in their principles; they are only terribly, tragically mistaken. And yet, as Shaw admits, there is comedy in that tragic conviction and in the clarity with which it is seen. One of Shaw's greatest comic gifts was to show the inevitable clash of impenetrable argumentative attitudes. In the trial-scene in *Saint Joan* he put that comic gift to the service of tragedy:

> *Cauchon*: . . . Joan: I am going to put a most solemn question to you. Take care how you answer; for your life and salvation are at stake on it. Will you for all you have said and done, be it good or bad, accept the judgement of God's Church on earth? More especially as to the acts and words that are imputed to you in this trial by the Promoter here, will you submit your case to the inspired interpretation of the Church Militant?
> *Joan*: I am a faithful child of the Church. I will obey the Church –
> *Cauchon* [*hopefully leaning forward*]: You will?
> *Joan*: – provided it does not command anything impossible.
> *Cauchon sinks back in his chair with a heavy sigh. The Inquisitor purses his lips and frowns. Ladvenu shakes his head pitifully.* (CP, VI, 173)

Joan's reply here is taken more or less directly from the trial transcript – 'On all that I am asked I will refer to the Church Militant, provided they do not command anything impossible.'[15] But Shaw in building up the solemnity of Cauchon's question, in breaking Joan's reply, makes of this a moment of anticlimax which is basically a comic technique. Joan cannot understand what seems so appallingly heretical to the judges in what she has said; the judges cannot for a moment enter into Joan's view of things. In another context we might be able to laugh; here the gap in understanding is too wide, the consequences too terrible, to make it a laughing matter.

Shaw talks of the tragedy of Joan's execution, coming after the

romance of her rise. Is it in fact tragedy as he represents it? It has
been a much argued question. The common view at the time of the
play's first production was that Shaw, for once, had written a true
tragedy, but had then ruined it by the addition of his comic
excrescence of an Epilogue. Arland Ussher has argued just the
opposite, that it is rather the burning of Joan which is anomalous,
out of key with the rest of the play and that the purpose of the
Epilogue is 'in fact, to restore the easy argumentative note which the
intrusion of the brutal historical facts has a little disturbed'.[16] This is
perhaps somewhat unfair – the clash of irreconcilable points of view
in the trial is in some sense experienced as a tragic clash – but it is
true to the extent that Shaw is unwilling to face the full horror of
Joan's execution. He could never bear really to imagine the idea of
pain, and one of the reasons that he opposed what he called
'Crosstianity' so vigorously was that he could not accept suffering as
redemptive. It is not accidental, therefore, that he chooses to register
the effect of the burning through the buffoon turned grotesque figure
of De Stogumber. The English Chaplain, the most vehement
opponent of Joan, who earlier declared his willingness to burn her
with his own hands, is utterly horrified by the sight itself. His broken
and hysterical words are intended to demonstrate the degree to
which cruelty is merely lack of imagination. But this is hardly a full
apprehension of the tragic nature of Joan's death, and Shaw keeps
De Stogumber's comic chauvinism to the end: 'Some of the people
laughed at her. They would have laughed at Christ. They were
French people, my lord: I know they were French' (CP, VI, 188). We
pity De Stogumber, we are even moved by his 'conversion', but we
are left with enough detachment to smile at his unconverted
partisanship.

From the moment of Joan's exit at the end of the trial, we can see
Shaw tuning the play back towards the serio-comic tone of the
Epilogue. Even the appearance of the Executioner involves a joke
(lifted directly from Shakespeare's Abhorson in *Measure for Measure*):

> *Warwick*: Well, fellow: who are you?
> *The Executioner* [*with dignity*]: I am not addressed as fellow, my
>   lord. I am the Master Executioner of Rouen: it is a highly
>   skilled mystery. (CP, VI, 190)

At certain moments Shaw is prepared to risk drastically lessening the
impact of the trial we have witnessed in order to achieve this re-

tuning of tone. As Cauchon is about to hurry out to stop the English dragging Joan straight to the stake without formal sentence by the secular authorities (as they in fact did), the Inquisitor holds him back: 'We have proceeded in perfect order. If the English choose to put themselves in the wrong, it is not our business to put them in the right. A flaw in the procedure may be useful later on: one never knows' (CP, VI, 185–6). There is a similar effect with the last line of the scene; when the Executioner assures Warwick that he has 'heard the last of her', he replies, 'The last of her? Hm! I wonder!' (CP, VI, 190). Shaw here prepares us for the reappearance of Joan in the Epilogue, prepares us for the continuation of her story into the 'comedy of the attempts of posterity to make amends' to her. But the knowingness of these lines given to the Inquisitor and to Warwick seems a real indecorum in context. The whole force of the trial-scene depends on the assumption that Joan's judges, and the Inquisitor especially, are men of complete probity. The suggestion that in fact the Inquisitor has one eye on the future when a technical loophole might be desirable, surely comes close to sabotaging altogether the integrity of the character. There is a theatrical slickness in Warwick's curtain-line which again seems to betray the seriousness of what we have just seen. Shaw's irresistible urge to turn his characters into smart-alecs rarely served him worse.

The Epilogue was essential to the play from Shaw's point of view: 'I could hardly be expected to stultify myself by implying that Joan's history in the world ended unhappily with her execution, instead of beginning there. It was necessary by hook or crook to shew the canonised Joan as well as the incinerated one' (CP, VI, 75). And hence we get a dream-sequence like that in *Man and Superman* with a similar comic eschatology: the Soldier describing the jolliness of Hell – 'Like as if you were always drunk without the trouble and expense of drinking. Tip top company too: emperors and popes and kings and all sorts' (CP, VI, 200). This vein of schoolboy facetiousness, so irritating and yet in a way rather endearing, is very characteristic of Shaw. The English soldier, in fact, had figured in his first fantastic sketch of what he might do with a 'Joan play' – 'beginning with the sweeping up of the cinders and orange peel *after* her martyrdom, and going on with Joan's arrival in heaven'.[17] The Epilogue is anti-tragic in that it allows us to escape the finality of death, so fundamental to the sense of tragedy, into a region of cosy immortality in which the characters can congregate amicably to discuss the action.

But the Epilogue is not merely Shaw the joker taking over after the self-restraint of the tragic drama. There is more to it than the opportunity for Joan to exchange bantering repartee with all the other characters, to give her shrewd comments on all that happened after her death. It is a real attempt to show Joan's tragedy in the ultimate light of divine comedy. The Epilogue is intended as a salute to the spirit of Joan and what it achieved both in the short term – the freeing of France, and the firm establishment of Charles VI on the throne – and in the long term – the inspiration to later generations recognised finally in the canonisation in 1920. This is formally expressed in the litany of praise from her assembled friends and enemies who kneel to her, in thanks for showing them their limitations. But this is followed by a deliberate anticlimax:

> *Joan:* . . . And now tell me: shall I rise from the dead, and come
> back to you a living woman,
> *A sudden darkness blots out the walls of the room as they all spring to
> their feet in consternation.* (CP, VI, 206)

One by one, in a pattern of denial to match the previous paean of praise, they refuse to accept the idea of her return. Shaw's design here is to repeat in little the basic structure of the play as a whole: the inspiring force of Joan which occupies the first half, met by the worldly sources which in the second half doom her to death. Projected on to a scale of eternal recurrence this figures what for Shaw is the ultimate tragedy of Joan, that the heroic can never be accepted in its own time, by implication the earth will never be ready to receive its saints.

'Joan of Arc as the subject of a historical hypothesis, as Shaw would have it, an exponent of certain ways of thinking – there is something annoying about it. In her irreducible uniqueness she can be understood only by means of a sense of sympathetic admiration.'[18] We may well be inclined to agree here with the medieval historian Johan Huizinga. For all the extraordinary skill of Shaw's dialectic in identifying Joan with emergent Protestantism and nationalism, there *is* something annoying about it. It is hard to repress a feeling that this is no more than Shavian cleverness. And yet, as Huizinga himself admits, what is remarkable is that Shaw did respond to Joan with the necessary 'sense of sympathetic admiration', was inspired by 'her irreducible uniqueness'. There was in this an element of personal identification with Joan, as many critics were quick to point out. Joan's single-mindedness, her militant spirit, her directness in cutting through forms and ceremonies to the heart of the matter, all of these were essentially congenial to Shaw. He may well also have been attracted to her asceticism and her chaste asexuality. Earlier playwrights had romanticised Joan's relationship with her followers, particularly La Hire. Shaw instead lays great emphasis on her fellow-soldiers who testified to her lack of sexual attractiveness. Joan at last gave Shaw a subject without what was for him the distracting nuisance of sex. Above all where he felt an affinity with Joan was in the capacity to be right when everyone else was wrong. There is a splendid anecdote told by Archibald Henderson – so well-turned that one suspects Shaw ghost-wrote it – about a lecture on Joan of Arc in which Shaw summed up all the various ways in which Joan 'knew everybody's business better than they knew it themselves'. He worked up to the deliberately provocative peroration: 'After pondering over the matter for a time, I finally hit upon the perfect word which exactly describes Joan: *insufferable*.' He got the reaction he was looking for from the lady who moved the vote of thanks, who pointed out 'the one fundamental error into which Mr Shaw had fallen: it is not Joan of Arc, but Mr Bernard Shaw who is insufferable'.[19] From Shaw's point of view, they were both insufferable because they told the truths that nobody wanted to hear. Arland Ussher sees an element of 'nostalgia' in this identification: 'The hero who is laughed at, tolerated, petted, cannot conceal a certain envy for the heroine who is taken seriously and killed.'[20] Perhaps – Shaw, though courageous enough, was not the stuff of which martyrs are made. But he was convinced that he was, like Joan, if not a martyr at least a witness to an understanding of the world which could only come after him. Whether or not this now seems like a delusion, it was a real emotional source for *Saint Joan*.

To emphasise the element of personal identification might be to suggest, what some people have felt, that what we get is really a Joan cut down to Shavian size. Negatively it is true that there are aspects of Jeanne d'Arc that Shaw could not engage with imaginatively and which he omits from his representation. One of the most poignant features of the trial transcript is Jeanne's repeated plea to be allowed to hear Mass, repeatedly refused except on the condition that she abandon her masculine dress. Although Shaw alludes to her devoutness in the Preface, this very Catholic need to participate in the ritual of the Mass could not be made part of his 'Protestant' Saint Joan. The certainty and resolution of Joan's faith were central for

Shaw. As a result he could not really render the moving sense of humility expressed in the phrase Jeanne used so frequently in the trial: 'I wait on Our Lord.' Shaw's religion is a rational irrationalism without mystery and in making Joan a saint of Creative Evolution, he could scarcely present her with the attributes of a canonised saint of the Roman Catholic Church. Hence the ambiguity of the treatment of the voices and the miracles. But Shaw's imagination did go out to Joan, he did dramatise something of the extraordinary quality of her life. *Saint Joan* may not be tragedy; there is a deliberateness, a clarity about its form and significance which seem to take away the sense of awe and bewilderment which tragedy at its most profound evokes. It may not be Shaw's greatest play. But his capacity to write it commands a special respect, and adds a dimension to his achievement as a playwright which it would otherwise have lacked. It helped him to deserve the Nobel Prize.

10 Language and Reality

To the common complaint that his plays were 'all talk', Shaw retorted, 'it is quite true that my plays are all talk, just as Raphael's pictures are all paint, Michael Angelo's statues all marble, Beethoven's symphonies are all noise'.[1] A deft defence. But the criticism is not quite as fatuous as Shaw makes it seem. His plays are made up, to a greater extent than those of other dramatists, of people talking – conversations, arguments, debates, repartee. A Shaw play, typically, began with the barest of scenarios, with a number of characters often without names in a given situation. From then on, as he said himself, he 'let them rip', that is he let them talk themselves into a dramatic shape. Speech is primary in Shavian drama – fluid, fluent, dexterous, eloquent speech. The charge that Shaw's characters are no more than talking heads may be unfair; his parts are fully and vividly realised, physically embodied on stage. But the process of dramatic imagination was for him in origin, and even in essence, a matter of the creation of voices in dialogue. If we are to define the peculiar nature of Shaw's dramatic reality, we need to try to analyse the nature of his language.

A look at Shaw's language may also be useful at this concluding stage of my study of the plays because it helps to place his work in perspective, to suggest in part why for so many late twentieth-century readers and critics Shaw should appear dated and out of fashion. Shaw wrote with a high confidence in his powers of expression, a confidence in language itself which few modern writers have shared. Eliot in 'Burnt Norton' evokes what has become our characteristic sense of the insecurity of words:

> Words strain,
> Crack, and sometimes break, under the burden,
> Under the tension, slip, slide, perish,
> Decay with imprecision, will not stay in place,
> Will not stay still.[2]

Our most prized literature and drama latterly has been concerned with the dysfunction of language, working always through indirection, ambiguity, the displacement of meaning. In this context Shaw's assured spate of language, in which there are no types of ambiguity, tends to be despised as shallow and unthinking. It is significant that Andrew Kennedy, in his highly illuminating study *Six Dramatists in Search of a Language*, diagnoses Shaw as 'premodern', not sufficiently aware of the 'sickness' that has fallen upon language, not critical or conscious enough to explore and exploit the modern crisis in language to find new forms of dramatic expression.[3]

If, however, we are to appreciate Shaw at all, we must not confuse fluency with facility, nor let ourselves be put off by his unfashionably unironical use of rhetoric. If Shaw's dramatic prose is rhetorical, it is a stage rhetoric unequalled in English. And it is very much a *stage* rhetoric. Nothing could be more mistaken than the old supposition that the long speeches which are so much a hallmark of Shavian drama are simply Shaw lectures transferred to the theatre. Shaw tasked his leading actors and actresses hard with the prodigious solos he wrote for them, but he knew exactly what he was doing and could give detailed instructions on how those solos were to be credibly performed. His long letter to J. L. Shine, for example (CL, II, 460–2), who was playing Larry Doyle in the first production of *John Bull's Other Island*, shows his subtle understanding of the transitions of mood, the underlying emotional contours of something like Larry's great 'dreaming' speech. (Both the speech and the commentary are unfortunately too long to quote.) Shine's reply is representative of the reaction of any number of actors whom Shaw directed: 'You are a man *worth* working for, and, if your brilliant play is not efficiently rendered, we alleged actors and actresses deserve extermination, for your Godlike patience and courteous consideration, combined with your skilful and workmanlike handling of detail, has been a revelation to me' (CL, II, 462). Shaw not only had a precise technical knowledge of the effects which he wanted to achieve with his speeches in the theatre, he was willing to trust the actors to find their own way of achieving those effects. During rehearsals of *Major Barbara* he wrote to Annie Russell, who was to create the title-role, of his reluctance to advise her on how to change her playing of a specific scene:

> unfortunately I am afraid to suggest anything as to your best way of handling it, because I do not know yet exactly how you get your

effects, except that it is not in my rather rhetorical, public-speaker kind of way. I may therefore quite easily set you wrong. . . . You have much greater resources in the direction of gentleness than I have; and I assure you you will go wrong every time you try to do what *I* like instead of letting yourself do what *you* like. A part that is any good can be played fifty different ways by fifty different people; so just assume that Barbara is yourself (not that you are Barbara) and let it come just as it takes you. (CL, II, 583)

What is involved here is more than merely respect for the actress's individuality; it is a belief in his own stage speeches as a living dramatic language.

One of the most helpful insights into Shaw's style is Martin Meisel's analysis of his debt to opera in the 'scoring' of his dialogue. Meisel shows how frequently Shaw's major scenes are duos, trios or quartets with a conscious counterpoint of voices of different register.[4] But it is no accident that Shaw's all-time favourite opera was *Don Giovanni*, for he exploits the operatic interplay of voices above all for comic effect. This, as much as the long speech, the rhetorical set-piece, is the special distinction of Shaw's dramatic dialogue. It has sometimes been complained that Shaw's characters all speak alike, that he does not give them really distinctive speech patterns of their own. That is true at least to the extent that he lends to a remarkable range of his characters his own articulateness, even eloquence. But the level of understanding represented by the speech of any given character is likely to be very different from the others, and it is from these divergent levels of understanding that Shaw creates his comic clash of voices. He is not concerned, as so many modern dramatists are, with the fragmentation and distortion of language representing the failure of communication. Instead he gives us people who can speak with incisive clarity but who fail to communicate none the less. His great comic talent lies in his capacity to bounce the speech of one character off another, to make the meaning of each crystal clear to us the audience, but unintelligible to one another.

Misapprehensions, malentendus, bathetic anticlimaxes are of the very stuff of Shaw's comedy. Richard Ohmann acutely demonstrates what he calls 'the uses of discontinuity' in Shaw's style and analyses the way in which his dialogue by its turns and shifts constantly frustrates linguistic expectations.[5] These cross purposes are rarely merely mechanical either; on the whole, Shaw does not deal in puns, for instance. An apparent exception illustrates the principle:

> *Raina*: . . . You must trust to our hospitality. You do not yet know
> in whose house you are. I am a Petkoff.
> *The Man*: A pet what? (CP, I, 407)

Raina's absurd snobbery is deflated by Bluntschli's prosaic
mishearing – a point is made. Rhetorical gestures, linguistic postur-
ing are constantly debunked by imperturbability, a key Shavian
characteristic. *Arms and the Man* again:

> *Sergius*: . . . Bluntschli: I have allowed you to call me a blockhead.
> You may now call me a coward as well. I refuse to fight you. Do
> you know why?
> *Bluntschli*: No; but it doesnt matter. I didnt ask the reason when
> you cried on; and I dont ask the reason now you cry off. (CP, I,
> 459–60)

But the anticlimactic and antiromantic denial of expected
emotional effects is only one way in which Shaw's comic crosstalk
works. The second act of *Candida* might be taken as an example of
the range of this technique. The act consists of a series of
conversations in which the characters talk past one another, each
with a complete and wholly misplaced confidence that their point of
view is shared with their interlocutor. Marchbanks apologises to
Proserpine Garnett, the secretary, for his assumption that she would
be familiar with love-letters:

> *Marchbanks*: I beg your pardon. I thought clever people – people
> who can do business and write letters and that sort of thing –
> always had to have love affairs to keep them from going mad.
> *Proserpine* [*rising, outraged*]: Mr Marchbanks! (CP, I, 548)

We see simultaneously what Marchbanks means and why Prossy is
conventionally scandalised. Then when Burgess is left alone with
Marchbanks, he speaks to him with an avuncular confidentiality
which is hilariously inappropriate. More seriously, later on, we have
Morell's bewildered disorientation as he listens to Candida in-
dependently echoing words which he has only recently heard from
Marchbanks spoken in a very different tone. Throughout the act,
the complacent incomprehension of Burgess is worked into a

recurring gag, as one by one he identifies all the other characters as mad. The self-assurance with which each character speaks, unaware of the effect that they are having, amounts almost to a comic solipsism. Shaw firmly believed that people could communicate through language, he had not a modernist's distrust of words. Yet some of his finest comedy derives from the obdurate incapacity of his characters to listen or understand.

And still, for all the real accomplishment of Shaw's dramatic dialogue, the dissatisfied impression of the talkiness of his characters persists. It is certainly not merely a recent reaction conditioned by the minimalist theatre of Beckett or Pinter, though that may be what makes the fluency of Shavian drama now seem unfashionable. Throughout Shaw's whole playwriting career it was the standard objection made to his work. There is more here, surely, than mere obtuse failure to understand the nature of his dramatic technique. Part of the difficulty may be the sense that Shaw's characters are unnaturally articulate, that, like Shaw himself, they seem never to be at a loss for words. This makes for a real restriction in the sort of characters he can convincingly represent. Dixon Scott put it well: 'for people who don't know their own minds and can't communicate the knowledge clearly, Shaw has no form of speech that will do. He can write nothing but definite dialogue; and definite dialogue entails definite minds.'[6] This is a real limitation, for Andrew Kennedy finally a crippling limitation: 'A language without power or silence, that seems to be the end of prose rhetoric in drama.'[7] To my mind this is mistaken in so far as it underestimates the very considerable power of Shaw's dramatic rhetoric, but the lack of silence is crucial. Shaw's basic technique prohibits him from penetrating into those areas of personality or experience which can only be expressed in the interstices of speech or in half-formed articulations which are no more than verbal gestures.

'It is the business of the stage to make its figures more intelligible to themselves than they would be in real life; for by no other means can they be made intelligible to the audience' (CP, VI, 73). This statement which I already quoted in the last chapter, for Edmund Wilson 'reads like a confession of limitation', a failure to understand 'character in action'.[8] But it also highlights how much it was Shaw's aim to make his characters and their speech above all *intelligible*. There is a much-quoted passage in the Epistle Dedicatory to *Man and Superman* in which Shaw argues that conviction alone forges style.

Effectiveness of assertion is the Alpha and Omega of style. He who has nothing to assert has no style and can have none: he who has something to assert will go as far in power of style as its momentousness and his conviction will carry him. (CP, II, 527)

In context we can see that this is partly overstated in opposition to the aesthetic doctrine which Shaw is out to combat: ' "for art's sake" alone I would not face the toil of writing a single sentence'. But it is true that for Shaw it is the message not the medium that matters, or at least that the medium should always subserve the message. Shaw is not concerned with language in and for itself, but always with language for what it says and does, as a tool, a precision implement.

This helps to explain Shaw's limitations in relation to poetry. The weakness of Shaw's attempts at poetic language, whether with Marchbanks or Dubedat or even Saint Joan, has frequently been demonstrated. In itself this might be accepted as a restriction in range which is hardly very important in a dramatist whose main idiom is prose comedy. In any case even the rather inadequate poetic speeches of Shaw can often work quite well in the theatre. His own lack of poetic capacity is significant rather as it relates to his understanding of poetry itself. Shaw was extremely sensitive to dramatic verse, as we can see, for example, in his letters to Ellen Terry advising her on the playing of Imogen which show a delicate responsiveness to nuance and intonation.[9] And yet he was capable of insisting that blank verse was 'childishly easy and expeditious' to write (CP, II, 433), or remarking that 'poetry is far too glib for my liking'.[10] The harmonies of poetry were seductive for Shaw, they seduced the reader away from meaning. This was the source of his wrangling relationship with Shakespeare whose 'word-music' he loved deeply and as deeply distrusted. At bottom poetry remained for him an art of rhetoric, which could be abused as decoration or used rightly in the service of meaning, but did not create meaning in itself.

Bruce Park has argued that this has been a major reason for the failure of modern critics to appreciate Shaw's work. 'To modern critics language is properly poetry; to Shaw language was properly prose.' This is well said and we may be inclined to agree with Park when he rebukes the critical misprision of Shaw: 'To read plays as though they ought to be poems or comedies as though they ought to be tragedies is surely a vulgar error.'[11] Other great playwrights, most notably Molière, to whom Shaw has so often been compared, have cultivated a language of precise and unambiguous meaning to express their comic vision. What is worrying with Shaw is his belief that comedy takes us closer to reality itself, that comic prose is ultimately a greater source of truth than tragic poetry. Keegan's apothegm – 'Every jest is an earnest in the womb of Time' – was no light paradox for Shaw. The comedian could be, was in his own case, a prophetic truth-teller, and the unillusioned prose style could pierce to the heart of the matter. It is this claim both for his comedy and his prose which we resist in Shaw, and surely rightly. Though comedy tells its own form of truth, it is by its acknowledged distortion of reality, by its deliberately mannered form of representation. Shaw could never see this about his own work, a delusion spotted already by Robert Louis Stevenson on reading *Cashel Byron's Profession*. In spite of the glorious fantasy of the novel, Stevenson said, 'I believe in his heart he thinks he is labouring in a quarry of solid granite realism'.[12]

The identification of truth with the clear, the demystified, the intelligible is one of the sources of our recurring sense of shallowness in Shaw. It implicitly denies both the plenitude of reality and of language used to express reality. It is the reason why comedies like *Arms and the Man* and *Pygmalion* seem all but flawless though they do not go very deep, whereas plays that go deeper – *Major Barbara* or *Heartbreak House* – leave us more doubtful and dissatisfied. It is here that the difference from Shakespeare makes itself so powerfully felt. In Shakespeare, even in the comedies, language may always evoke a quite unexpected dimension of reality. In *All's Well that Ends Well* (one of Shaw's favourite Shakespeare plays), after the humiliation of Parolles, the buoyancy of the comic character is transformed into a very human sense of survival:

> Captain I'll be no more
> But I will eat and drink, and sleep as soft
> As captain shall: simply the thing I am
> Shall make me live. (IV, iii, 336–9)

The great speech of Shylock, 'Hath not a Jew eyes', erupts into a scene of highly patterned comedy in which Shylock is the butt. It derives, one suspects, not from any predetermined pro-Semitism on Shakespeare's part, but from living words welling up out of the life of the imagined character. There are no moments quite like this in Shaw. Unexpected shifts in our viewpoint of Shavian characters are visibly part of an over-all dramatic strategy, manipulated from without rather than emerging from within. And thus our final impression of Shaw's dramatic world, for all the extraordinary vividness of his characterisation and the supple skills of his stage language, is of men and women without shadows, of voices without echoes.

Notes

Preface

1. A. M. Gibbs, *The Art and Mind of Shaw* (London, 1983) p. 39.
2. Martin Meisel, *Shaw and the Nineteenth-Century Theater* (Princeton, 1963).
3. See Robert F. Whitman, *Shaw and the Play of Ideas* (Ithaca, N.Y., 1977), Leon Hugo, *Bernard Shaw: Playwright and Preacher* (London, 1971) and Irving Wardle, 'The Plays' in *The Genius of Shaw*, ed. Michael Holroyd (London, 1979).
4. Eric Bentley, *Bernard Shaw: a Reconsideration* (New York, rev. edn 1957) p. xxi.

Chapter 1: Two Models: Wilde and Ibsen

1. For a very interesting discussion of the question see Thomas Kilroy, 'Anglo-Irish playwrights and comic tradition', *The Crane Bag*, III, no. 2 (1979) 19–27.
2. *The Critical Writings of James Joyce*, ed. Ellsworth Mason and Richard Ellmann (London, 1959) p. 202.
3. Bernard Shaw, *Our Theatres in the Nineties*, I (London, 1931) pp. 10–11.
4. Ibid., p. 44.
5. Ibid., pp. 44–5.
6. *The Playwright and the Pirate: Bernard Shaw and Frank Harris. A Correspondence*, ed. Stanley Weintraub (Gerrards Cross, Bucks, 1982) p. 33.
7. Bernard Shaw, *The Matter with Ireland*, ed. Dan H. Laurence and David H. Greene (New York, 1962) p. 31.
8. Ibid., p. 32.
9. Ibid., p. 29.
10. For the significance of Ibsen's work and Shaw's *Quintessence of Ibsenism* in the formation of the Shavian dialectic, see particularly J. L. Wisenthal, *The Marriage of Contraries: Bernard Shaw's Middle Plays* (Toronto, 1974), and Alfred Turco Jr, *Shaw's Moral Vision: the Self and Salvation* (Ithaca, N.Y., 1976).
11. *Shaw and Ibsen: Bernard Shaw's* The Quintessence of Ibsenism *and Related Writings*, ed. J. L. Wisenthal (Toronto, 1979).
12. Letter to Frederik Hegel, dated 23 November 1881, quoted in *The Oxford Ibsen*, v, trans. and ed. James Walter McFarlane (London, 1961) p. 474.
13. Margery M. Morgan, *The Shavian Playground* (London, 1972) pp. 87–9.
14. See Shaw's letter to William Archer of 7 September 1903 (CL, II, 362–3), and a chapter contributed by Shaw to Cyril Maude's *The Haymarket Theatre* (reprinted in CP, I, 797–803).
15. Tolstoy wrote to Shaw reproaching him for the comic tone of *Man and*

Superman: 'you are not sufficiently serious. One should not speak jokingly about such a subject as the purpose of human life or the causes of its perversion and of the evil that fills the life of all of us mankind'. *Tolstoy's Letters*, II, ed. and trans. R. F. Christian (New York, 1978) p. 678.

16. Wisenthal, *Shaw and Ibsen*, p. 243.
17. See my *Shakespeare, Jonson, Molière: the Comic Contract* (London, 1980).

Chapter 2: Pleasant/Unpleasant

1. As was demonstrated in the successful London National Theatre production of 1978–9.
2. Charles Shattuck compares the 1893 and the 1898 texts in 'Bernard Shaw's bad Quarto', *Journal of English and Germanic Philology*, 54 (1955) 651–63.
3. The quotation here, and throughout, is from the text of Shaw's final revision in 1930, but it is not substantially different from the 1898 *Plays Unpleasant* text.
4. Preface to *Miss Julie* – August Strindberg, *The Plays*, I, trans. and ed. Michael Meyer (London, rev. edn, 1975) p. 101.
5. See Frank Harris, *Bernard Shaw* (London, 1931) and, most recently, Arnold Silver, *Bernard Shaw: the Darker Side* (Stanford, Calif., 1982).
6. The play was apparently fairly directly based on Shaw's relationship with Jenny Patterson (Julia Craven) and Florence Farr (Grace Tranfield). For details see, for instance, Dan H. Laurence's note in CL, I, 295–6.
7. 'I have removed with the greatest care every line that could provoke a smile' (CP, I, 127). See above, p. 2.
8. Bernard Shaw, *Mrs Warren's Profession: a Facsimile of the Holograph Manuscript*, ed. Margot Peters (New York, 1981) pp. 204–6, 252–5.
9. In draft Vivie has an even more explicit speech: 'Frank was the most unbearable thought of all, for I knew that he would force on me the sort of relation that my mother's life had tainted for ever for me. I felt that I would rather die than let him touch me with that in his mind.' Ibid., p. 205.
10. Eric Bentley, *Bernard Shaw: a Reconsideration*, p. 107.
11. Charles Carpenter, *Bernard Shaw and the Art of Destroying Ideals* (Madison, Wis., 1969) p. 58. Martin Meisel, also, sees Vivie as 'formidable but seared and maimed' in the end, 'Shaw and revolution: the politics of the plays' in *Shaw: Seven Critical Essays*, ed. Norman Rosenblood (Toronto, 1971) p. 118.
12. Margery Morgan, *The Shavian Playground*, Chapter 3.
13. Louis Crompton helpfully suggests that 'Shaw is using the term "Pre-Raphaelite" as synonymous with "neomediaeval" and . . . he deliberately lumps together under this one term not only the art movement usually designated by it but also such varied social and religious phenomena as Christian Socialism and Anglo-Catholicism', *Shaw the Dramatist* (London, 1971) p. 32.
14. 'The play is a counterblast to Ibsen's Doll's House, showing that in the real typical doll's house it is the man who is the doll' (CP, I, 603).
15. Arthur H. Nethercot is Candida's severest critic – *Men and Supermen: the Shavian Portrait Gallery* (Cambridge, Mass., 1954). Among her more recent defenders are Charles Carpenter and Margery Morgan.
16. See Morgan, *The Shavian Playground*, pp. 81–2.

17. *Our Theatres in the Nineties*, i, p. vi.
18. See, for example, his letter to Lady Gregory about *The Shewing-up of Blanco Posnet:* 'All this problem of the origin of evil, the mystery of pain, and so forth, does not puzzle me. My doctrine is that God proceeds by the method of "trial and error", just like a workman perfecting an aeroplane' (CL, ii, 858).

Chapter 3: Stage Tricks and Suspenses

1. Martin Meisel, *Shaw and the Nineteenth-Century Theater.*
2. See Shaw's letter to Ellen Terry, CL, i, 572.
3. See Meisel, p. 361.
4. Bernard Shaw, *The Devil's Disciple : a Facsimile of the Holograph Manuscript*, ed. Robert F. Whitman (New York, 1981) p. 27.
5. Ibid., p. 195.
6. Maurice Valency, *The Cart and the Trumpet* (New York, 1973) p. 167.
7. *Our Theatres in the Nineties*, i, p. 93.
8. See Meisel, pp. 198–200.
9. Margery Morgan, *The Shavian Playground*, p. 240.
10. It seems that Shaw took his cue for some of his idealisation of Caesar from Mommsen, the nineteenth-century Roman historian, but he whitewashes Caesar even more thoroughly than Mommsen. See Gordon W. Couchman, 'Here was a Caesar: Shaw's comedy today', *PMLA*, LXXII (1957) 272–85.
11. When the play was given its first production in German in 1906, Max Reinhardt disregarded Shaw's instructions to cut the third act. Shaw's indignation is recorded in his letter to Siegfried Trebitsch, CL, ii, 619–20.

Chapter 4: Comedy and Dialectic

1. *Shaw: the Critical Heritage*, ed. T. F. Evans (London, 1976) p. 103.
2. The most recent revival of the whole play was an excellent production by the National Theatre in London in 1981.
3. For details of the study of the sources of *Man and Superman*, see Stanley Weintraub's chapter on Shaw in Richard J. Finneran (ed.), *Anglo-Irish Literature: a Review of Research* (New York, 1976) pp. 191–2.
4. Arthur Schopenhauer, *The World as Will and Idea*, trans. R. B. Haldane and J. Kemp, vol. iii (London, 1886). Schopenhauer's influence on Shaw's thinking in *Man and Superman* has been discussed by Louis Crompton, *Shaw the Dramatist*, pp. 84–5, 88–9, and by Maurice Valency, *The Cart and the Trumpet*, pp. 203–5.
5. The tone and attitude of the 'Metaphysics of the Love of the Sexes' seems strikingly different from Schopenhauer's essay 'On Women', which also had its effect on Shaw's *Man and Superman*. Schopenhauer's comment on women's 'irremediable tendency to lying' reads like a gloss on Ann Whitefield. See *Selected Essays of Arthur Schopenhauer*, ed. Ernest Belfort Bax (London, 1891).
6. Alfred Turco Jr points out in *Shaw's Moral Vision*, p. 160, that the Life Force is not Bergson's *élan vital*: Bergson's *L'Evolution Créatrice* did not appear until four years after *Man and Superman*.
7. Quoted by Martin Meisel, *Shaw and the Nineteenth-Century Theater*, p. 54.

8. Maurice Valency, *The Cart and the Trumpet*, pp. 200ff.
9. Charles A. Berst, *Bernard Shaw and the Art of Drama* (Urbana, Ill., 1973) p. 128, suggests that *Don Juan in Hell* is 'second cousin to Strindberg's dream plays, implicitly centred, as they are, in a single dreaming consciousness, and developed in large part through the rambling associations of the consciousness'.
10. I have been unable to find definite evidence for the extent of Shaw's knowledge of Plato, but from the pattern of references in his letters and published works it would seem likely that he knew Plato only at second-hand up until the beginning of 1899, that at some point around then he read *The Republic* which is an influence not only on *Man and Superman* (1901–2), but on *Major Barbara* (1905). There are fewer detailed references to Plato in later years, but they seem all to be allusions to *The Republic*.
11. See 'Giving the Devil his due', in *Pen Portraits and Reviews* (London, 1931) pp. 229–31.
12. Robert F. Whitman, *Shaw and the Play of Ideas*, p. 171.
13. Louis Crompton, *Shaw the Dramatist*, pp. 82–3.
14. See, among others, Charles Berst, *Bernard Shaw and the Art of Drama*.

Chapter 5: A Geographical Conscience

1. See, for example, Alfred Turco Jr, *Shaw's Moral Vision*, pp. 175–92.
2. See Frederick P. W. McDowell, 'Politics, Comedy, Character and Dialectic: the Shavian World of *John Bull's Other Island*', *PMLA*, 82 (1967) 542–53.
3. M. J. Sidnell relates the play to *Candida* in 'Hic and Ille: Shaw and Yeats' in *Theatre and Nationalism in Twentieth-century Ireland*, ed. Robert O'Driscoll (Toronto, 1971) pp. 156–78; among the critics who have compared *John Bull* to *Major Barbara* is J. L. Wisenthal, *The Marriage of Contraries*.
4. *The Letters of W. B. Yeats*, ed. Allan Wade (London, 1954) p. 335.
5. See *Bernard Shaw's Letters to Granville Barker*, ed. C. B. Purdom (London, 1956) pp. 22–40.
6. This letter was originally published by M. J. Sidnell in '*John Bull's Other Island* – Yeats and Shaw', *Modern Drama*, XI (1968) 245–51, and reprinted in his expanded version of this article cited above. It is also reproduced in T. F. Evans, *Shaw: the Critical Heritage*, pp. 122–4.
7. Quoted by Lady Gregory, *Our Irish Theatre* (New York, 1913) p. 9.
8. Cf. Joseph M. Hassett, 'Climate and character in *John Bull's Other Island*', *Shaw: The Annual of Bernard Shaw Studies*, ed. Stanley Weintraub, II (1982) 17–25.
9. See James Joyce, *Letters*, III, ed. Richard Ellmann (London, 1966) p. 50.
10. W. R. Beard, *Shaw's* John Bull's Other Island: *a critical, historical and theatrical study*, doctoral dissertation, University of London, 1974, p. 226.
11. Reported in Yeats's letter to Shaw.
12. McDowell, 'Politics, comedy, character and dialectic', 549.
13. It is interesting that Broadbent's Heaven was based on a dream of Shaw's as a child. See Hesketh Pearson, *Bernard Shaw* (London, 1961) p. 23.
14. T. F. Evans, *Shaw: the Critical Heritage*, p. 133.

Chapter 6: Giving the Devil More Than His Due

1. See Louis Crompton, *Shaw the Dramatist*, pp. 105–7.
2. T. F. Evans, *Shaw: the Critical Heritage*, p. 160.
3. See Bernard F. Dukore's introduction to *Major Barbara: a Facsimile of the Holograph Manuscript* (New York, 1981) for a detailed account of the play's composition.
4. Peter Ure, 'Master and Pupil in Bernard Shaw', *Yeats and Anglo-Irish Literature*, ed. C. J. Rawson (Liverpool, 1974) p. 269.
5. Desmond MacCarthy, *Shaw* (London, 1951) p. 48.
6. Bernard Dukore, *Major Barbara*, p. 2.
7. James Walter McFarlane, *The Oxford Ibsen*, v, p. 384.
8. See Maurice Valency, *The Cart and the Trumpet*, pp. 249–52, and Stanley Weintraub, *The Unexpected Shaw* (New York, 1982) pp. 151–3.
9. Eric Bentley, *Bernard Shaw: a Reconsideration*, p. 31.
10. See Charles Frankel, 'Efficient Power and Inefficient Virtue', in *Great Moral Dilemmas in Literature, Past and Present*, ed. R. M. McIver (New York, 1956) pp. 15–23.

Chapter 7: The Perfection of Levity

1. *Ellen Terry and Bernard Shaw*, ed. Christopher St. John (London, 3rd edn, 1949) p. 234.
2. Peter Ure, 'Master and pupil in Bernard Shaw', in *Yeats and Anglo-Irish Literature*, p. 269.
3. The relation between play and film version has raised textual problems for critics of *Pygmalion*. When Shaw revised the play in 1941 for the Standard Edition text, he included in it a number of scenes originally written for the film. Some critics have argued that these film episodes weaken rather than add to the impact of the play and have therefore returned to the stage version printed in the collection *Androcles and the Lion, Overruled, Pygmalion* (1916). I would agree that the additional scenes contribute very little and I have largely ignored them in this chapter. However I have followed the Bodley Head Bernard Shaw text which is based on the 1941 revision, rather than the 1916 version, because it includes changes in the dialogue and stage directions which have nothing to do with the film, but represent Shaw's usual practice of sharpening dramatic effects in revision.
4. Bernard Shaw, *The Intelligent Woman's Guide to Socialism and Capitalism* (London, 1928) p. 201.
5. Louis Crompton, *Shaw the Dramatist*, p. 146. Eric Bentley is equally critical – 'Doolittle commits the cardinal sin on the Shavian scale – he is irresponsible' – *Bernard Shaw: A Reconsideration*, p. 126.
6. *Androcles and the Lion, Overruled, Pygmalion* (London, 1916) p. 115.
7. See the detailed account of the making of the film in Bernard F. Dukore's Introduction to *The Collected Screenplays of Bernard Shaw* (London, 1980) pp. 65–88.
8. Ibid., p. 226.

9. St John Ervine is one of the firmest exponents of this view; see his *Bernard Shaw: His Life, Work and Friends* (London, 1956) p. 460.

10. See Phillip Weissmann, *Creativity in the Theatre* (London, 1965), and Arnold Silver, *Bernard Shaw: the Darker Side*.

11. *Bernard Shaw: a Reconsideration*, p. 125.

12. *Shaw the Dramatist*, p. 148.

Chapter 8: Bangs and Whimpers

1. 'Bernard Shaw: the Face Behind the Mask', reprinted from *The Theatre of Revolt* in R. J. Kaufmann (ed.), *G.B. Shaw: a Collection of Critical Essays* (Englewood Cliffs, N.J., 1965) pp. 100–18.

2. Francis Fergusson, *The Idea of a Theater* (Princeton, 1949) p. 182.

3. It is Stanley Weintraub who has made the case for this view of the play most fully in *Bernard Shaw 1914–1918: Journey to Heartbreak* (London, 1973), but it is implicit in the approach of other critics.

4. Alfred Turco Jr, *Shaw's Moral Vision: the Self and Salvation*, p. 253.

5. Middleton Murry's review, which originally appeared in the *Athenaeum*, is included in T. F. Evans, *Shaw: the Critical Heritage*, p. 246.

6. See, for instance, J. L. Styan's glancing reference to it as a 'rag-bag of a play' in *The Dark Comedy* (Cambridge, 2nd edn, 1968) p. 128.

7. Turco, *Shaw's Moral Vision*, p. 232; but see also Margery Morgan, *The Shavian Playground*, pp. 201–2.

8. Shaw originally gave 1913–1916 as the dates of the play's composition, but Stanley Weintraub and Anne Wright show that it was actually written between 4 March 1916 and May 1917: see their introduction to Bernard Shaw, *Heartbreak House, a Facsimile of the Revised Typescript* (New York, 1981).

9. Alan Dent (ed.), *Bernard Shaw and Mrs Patrick Campbell: Their Correspondence* (London, 1952) p. 186.

10. See Weintraub and Wright, Introduction, op. cit.

11. Ibid., p. 76.

12. Ibid., p. 163.

13. Evans, *Shaw: the Critical Heritage*, p. 239.

14. Weintraub and Wright, pp. 28, 47.

15. Weintraub, *Bernard Shaw 1914–1918*, p. 165.

16. Desmond MacCarthy, *Shaw*, p. 144.

17. St John Ervine, *Bernard Shaw: His life, Work and Friends*, p. 453.

18. *Bernard Shaw and Mrs Patrick Campbell*, p. 198.

19. Weintraub and Wright, Introduction, p. xvi.

20. Weintraub, *Bernard Shaw 1914–1918*, p. 179.

21. *Shaw*, p. 144.

22. Weintraub and Wright, p. 9.

Chapter 9: Shavian History

1. T. S. Eliot, 'Tradition and the individual talent', in *The Sacred Wood* (London, 1920) p. 52.

2. This three-part division of the play is noticed also by Eric Bentley, *Bernard Shaw: a Reconsideration*, p. 172.

3. Quoted by Brian Tyson, *The Story of Shaw's* Saint Joan (Kingston and Montreal, 1982) p. 19.

4. T. Douglas Murray (ed.), *Jeanne d'Arc. Maid of Orleans, Deliverer of France. Being the Story of her Life, her Achievements, and her Death, as attested on Oath and Set Forth in the Original Documents* (London, 1902). See Brian Tyson, op. cit.

5. Bentley, p. 171.

6. Louis Crompton, *Shaw the Dramatist*, p. 257. (Crompton's chapter on *Saint Joan* is in other ways very helpful and illuminating.)

7. Dame Sybil Thorndike, 'Thanks to Bernard Shaw' in Raymond Mander and Joe Mitchenson, *Theatrical Companion to Shaw* (London, 1954) p. 14.

8. Desmond MacCarthy, *Shaw*, p. 163.

9. Murray, p. xvii.

10. Ibid., pp. 82, 86.

11. See Tyson, p. 4.

12. Robert F. Whitman, *Shaw and the Play of Ideas*, p. 270.

13. Tyson, p. 46, quotes the Ibsen lines in the William Archer translation which would, of course, have been the one familiar to Shaw.

14. Murray, p. xv.

15. Ibid., p. 103.

16. Arland Ussher, *Three Great Irishmen* (New York, 1953) p. 32.

17. *Bernard Shaw and Mrs Patrick Campbell*, p. 146.

18. Johan Huizinga, 'Bernard Shaw's Saint' in *Men and Ideas: History, the Middle Ages, the Renaissance*, trans. James S. Holmes and Hans van Marle (London, 1959) p. 238.

19. Archibald Henderson, *Bernard Shaw: Playboy and Prophet* (New York, 1932) pp. 694–5.

20. Ussher, p. 33.

Chapter 10: Language and Reality

1. 'The Play of Ideas', in *Shaw on Theatre*, ed. E. J. West (London, 1958) p. 290.

2. T. S. Eliot, *Collected Poems* (London, 1963) p. 194.

3. Andrew Kennedy, *Six Dramatists in Search of a Language* (Cambridge, 1975).

4. Martin Meisel, *Shaw and the Nineteenth-Century Theater*, pp. 50–5.

5. Richard M. Ohmann, *Shaw: the Style and the Man* (Middletown, Conn., 1962). This very interesting book unfortunately concentrates mainly on Shaw's non-dramatic prose, but the chapter on 'The Uses of Discontinuity' includes an analysis of an extended passage from *The Devil's Disciple*, pp. 48–53.

6. Dixon Scott, 'The innocence of Bernard Shaw', *Men of Letters* (London, 1916) p. 42.

7. Kennedy, p. 83.

8. Edmund Wilson, 'Bernard Shaw since the war', reprinted as '*Saint Joan*: The unexpected in Shaw', in *Saint Joan Fifty Years After: 1923/4–1973/4*, ed. Stanley Weintraub (Baton Rouge, Louisiana, 1973) p. 43.

9. *Ellen Terry and Bernard Shaw: a correspondence*, pp. 42–58.

10. Quoted by Bruce R. Park, 'A mote in the critic's eye: Bernard Shaw and comedy', included in *G. B. Shaw: a collection of critical essays*, ed. R. J. Kaufmann, p. 48.
11. Ibid., pp. 49, 56.
12. *The Letters of Robert Louis Stevenson*, II, ed. Sidney Colvin (London, 1899) pp. 92–3.

Bibliography

Works by Shaw (abbreviations used in square brackets)

Androcles and the Lion, Overruled, Pygmalion (London, 1916).
Bernard Shaw and Mrs Patrick Campbell: their Correspondence, ed. Alan Dent (London, 1952).
Bernard Shaw's Letters to Granville Barker, ed. C. B. Purdom (London, 1956).
The Bodley Head Bernard Shaw: Collected Plays with Their Prefaces, 7 vols (London 1970–4) [CP, I–VII].
Collected Letters 1874–1897, ed. Dan H. Laurence (London, 1965) [CL, I].
Collected Letters 1898–1910, ed. Dan H. Laurence (London, 1972) [CL, II].
The Collected Screenplays of Bernard Shaw, ed. Bernard F. Dukore (London, 1980).
The Devil's Disciple: a Facsimile of the Holograph Manuscript, Introduction by Robert F. Whitman (New York, 1981).
Ellen Terry and Bernard Shaw: a Correspondence, ed. Christopher St. John (London, 3rd edn, 1949).
Heartbreak House: a Facsimile of the Revised Typescript, Introduction by Stanley Weintraub and Anne Wright (New York, 1981).
The Intelligent Woman's Guide to Socialism and Capitalism (London, 1928).
Major Barbara: a Facsimile of the Holograph Manuscript, Introduction by Bernard F. Dukore (New York, 1981).
The Matter with Ireland, ed. Dan H. Laurence and David H. Greene (New York, 1962).
Mrs Warren's Profession: a Facsimile of the Holograph Manuscript, Introduction by Margot Peters (New York, 1981).
Our Theatres in the Nineties, 3 vols (London, 1931).
Pen Portraits and Reviews (London, 1931).
The Playwright and the Pirate. Bernard Shaw and Frank Harris: a

Correspondence, ed. Stanley Weintraub (Gerrards Cross, Bucks, 1982).

Shaw on Theatre, ed. E. J. West (London, 1958).

Other References Cited

Ernest Belfort Bax (ed.), *Selected Essays of Arthur Schopenhauer* (London, 1891).

W. R. Beard, *Shaw's 'John Bull's Other Island': a Critical, Historical and Theatrical Study*, doctoral dissertation, University of London, 1974.

Eric Bentley, *Bernard Shaw: a Reconsideration* (New York, rev. edn, 1957).

Charles A. Berst, *Bernard Shaw and the Art of Drama* (Urbana, Ill., 1973).

Charles A. Carpenter, *Bernard Shaw and the Art of Destroying Ideals* (Madison, Wis., 1969).

R. F. Christian (ed.) *Tolstoy's Letters*, 2 vols (New York, 1978).

Sidney Colvin (ed.), *The Letters of Robert Louis Stevenson*, 2 vols (London, 1899).

Gordon W. Couchman, 'Here was a Caesar: Shaw's comedy today', *PMLA*, 72 (1957) 272–85.

Louis Crompton, *Shaw the Dramatist* (London, 1971).

T. S. Eliot, *Collected Poems* (London, 1963).

——, *The Sacred Wood* (London, 1920).

St John Ervine, *Bernard Shaw: His Life, Work and Friends* (London, 1956).

T. F. Evans (ed.), *Shaw: the Critical Heritage* (London, 1976).

Francis Fergusson, *The Idea of a Theater* (Princeton, 1949).

Richard J. Finneran (ed.), *Anglo-Irish Literature: a Review of Research* (New York, 1976).

A. M. Gibbs, *The Art and Mind of Shaw* (London, 1983).

Lady Augusta Gregory, *Our Irish Theatre* (New York, 1913).

Nicholas Grene, *Shakespeare, Jonson, Molière: the Comic Contract* (London, 1980).

Frank Harris, *Bernard Shaw* (London, 1931).

Joseph M. Hassett, 'Climate and character in *John Bull's Other Island*', *Shaw: the Annual of Bernard Shaw Studies*, II (1982) 17–25.

Archibald Henderson, *Bernard Shaw: Playboy and Prophet* (New York, 1932).

Michael Holroyd (ed.), *The Genius of Shaw* (London, 1979).

Leon Hugo, *Bernard Shaw: Playwright and Preacher* (London, 1971).

Johan Huizinga, *Men and Ideas: History, the Middle Ages, the Renaissance*, trans. James S. Holmes and Hans van Marle (London, 1959).

James Joyce, *Letters*, III, ed. Richard Ellmann (London, 1966).

R. J. Kaufmann (ed.), *G. B. Shaw: a Collection of Critical Essays* (Englewood Cliffs, N.J., 1965).

Andrew Kennedy, *Six Dramatists in Search of a Language* (Cambridge, 1975).

Thomas Kilroy, 'Anglo-Irish playwrights and comic tradition', *The Crane Bag*, III, no. 2. (1979) 19–27.

Desmond MacCarthy, *Shaw* (London, 1951).

Frederick P. W. McDowell, 'Politics, comedy, character, and dialectic: the Shavian world of *John Bull's Other Island*', *PMLA*, 82 (1967) 542–53.

James Walter McFarlane (ed.), *The Oxford Ibsen*, V (London, 1961).

R. M. McIver (ed.), *Great Moral Dilemmas in Literature, Past and Present* (New York, 1956).

Raymond Mander and Joe Mitchenson, *Theatrical Companion to Shaw* (London, 1954).

Ellsworth Mason and Richard Ellmann (eds.), *The Critical Writings of James Joyce* (London, 1959).

Martin Meisel, *Shaw and the Nineteenth-Century Theater* (Princeton, 1963).

Margery M. Morgan, *The Shavian Playground* (London, 1972).

T. Douglas Murray, *Jeanne D'Arc Maid of Orléans, Deliverer of France: Being the Story of her Life, her Achievements, and her Death, as attested on Oath and Set forth in the Original Documents* (London, 1902).

Arthur H. Nethercot, *Men and Supermen: the Shavian Portrait Gallery* (Cambridge, Mass., 1954).

Robert O'Driscoll (ed.), *Theatre and Nationalism in Twentieth-Century Ireland* (Toronto, 1971).

Richard M. Ohmann, *Shaw: the Style and the Man* (Middletown, Conn., 1962).

Hesketh Pearson, *Bernard Shaw* (London, 1961).

Norman Rosenblood (ed.), *Shaw: Seven Critical Essays* (Toronto, 1971).

Arthur Schopenhauer, *The World as Will and Idea*, III, trans. R. B. Haldane and J. Kemp (London, 1886).

Dixon Scott, *Men of Letters* (London, 1916).

Charles Shattuck, 'Bernard Shaw's Bad Quarto', *Journal of English and Germanic Philology*, 54 (1955) 651–63.

M. J. Sidnell, '*John Bull's Other Island*: Yeats and Shaw', *Modern Drama*, XI (1968) 245–51.

Arnold Silver, *Bernard Shaw: the Darker Side* (Stanford, Calif., 1982).

August Strindberg, *The Plays*, I, trans. and ed. Michael Meyer (London, rev. edn, 1975).

J. L. Styan, *The Dark Comedy* (Cambridge, 2nd edn, 1968).

Alfred Turco Jr, *Shaw's Moral Vision: the Self and Salvation* (Ithaca, N.Y., 1976).

Brian Tyson, *The Story of Shaw's* Saint Joan (Kingston and Montreal, 1982).

Peter Ure, *Yeats and Anglo-Irish Literature*, ed. C. J. Rawson (Liverpool, 1974).

Arland Ussher, *Three Great Irishmen* (New York, 1953).

Maurice Valency, *The Cart and the Trumpet* (New York, 1973).

Allan Wade (ed.), *The Letters of W. B. Yeats* (London, 1954).

Stanley Weintraub, *Bernard Shaw 1914–1918: Journey to Heartbreak* (London, 1973).

——, *Saint Joan Fifty Years After: 1923/4–1973/4* (Baton Rouge, Louisiana, 1973).

——, *The Unexpected Shaw* (New York, 1982).

Phillip Weissmann, *Creativity in the Theatre* (London, 1965).

Robert F. Whitman, *Shaw and the Play of Ideas* (Ithaca, N.Y., 1977).

J. L. Wisenthal, *The Marriage of Contraries: Bernard Shaw's Middle Plays* (Cambridge, Mass., 1974).

——, *Shaw and Ibsen: Bernard Shaw's* The Quintessence of Ibsenism *and Related Writings* (Toronto, 1979).

Index